Company Boards

By the same author

Social Policies for Old Age (1957)
Security of Employment: A Study in the
  Construction Industry (1968)
Company Giving (1969)

COMPANY BOARDS

Their Responsibilities to Shareholders,
Employees, and the Community

PEP
Political and Economic Planning
12 Upper Belgrave Street

Barbara Estelle Shenfield

London · George Allen & Unwin Ltd
Ruskin House · Museum Street

Printed in Great Britain
in 10 point Times Roman type
by W. & J. Mackay & Co Ltd, Chatham

Acknowledgements

This book is the product of a three-year study undertaken by Mrs Barbara Shenfield and financed by a grant from the Social Science Research Council. The study is part of a wider programme of research carried out at PEP into the nature of the modern corporation, which has resulted in a number of other publications that are listed below.

Mrs Shenfield was assisted by Mrs Janet Moore in the research for Chapter 2, and by Mrs Diana Landry in general secretarial work and in statistical help for Chapter 2.

Many firms and individuals gave help without which the study could not have been successfully undertaken. The co-operation of the firms where case studies were made was particularly far-reaching and helpful. A number of Chairmen, other Directors and Company Secretaries provided valuable interviews with Mrs Shenfield, and a score of firms gave substantial time to the completion of a questionnaire. Very many others gave useful advice and information in connection with the study. Members of the Advisory Group, in particular, read the numerous drafts connected with the whole programme of studies and gave invaluable guidance and advice. To all of these PEP and the author are most grateful. Responsibility for the opinions expressed is, however, that of the author alone.

LIST OF PEP PUBLICATIONS ON THE MODERN CORPORATION AND COMPANY LAW

The Company: Law, Structure and Reform in Eleven Countries, edited by Charles de Hoghton, published by George Allen & Unwin, 1970.

Cross-Channel Collaboration, by Charles de Hoghton, published by PEP, 1967.

Companies Beyond Jenkins, by M. Fogarty, published by PEP, Broadsheet No. 486, 1965.

Wider Business Objectives: American thinking and experience, by M. Fogarty, published by PEP, Broadsheet No. 495, 1966.

A Companies Act 1970? by M. Fogarty, published by PEP, Broadsheet No. 500, 1967.

The Control of Company Fraud, by T. Hadden, published by PEP, Broadsheet No. 503, 1968.

The Proposal for a European Company, by Dennis Thompson, published by PEP and Chatham House, European Series No. 13, 1969.

Contents

Introduction

Company Accountability: the demand for changes in Company Law and Practice

The need for a redefinition of the responsibilities of company boards in order to bring law and practice into consonance has been debated fairly continuously since studies of the modern corporation[1] first drew attention forty years ago to the gap in accountability opened up by the increasing divorce between ownership and control of companies. Many proposals for the reform of company law and practice have since been canvassed which their advocates claim would establish a more acceptable balance between the unfettered discretion of directors to manage, and their control by those whose interests the company is supposed to serve. However, neither in 1948 nor in 1967/8 when Company Law was amended was a satisfactory substitute found for shareholders as the focus for company accountability. Thus the recent growth of takeovers, mergers, conglomerates and multinational corporations has only drawn attention again to a well-known difficulty. Is it inevitable that numerous and widely dispersed shareholders will be unable and unwilling to exercise their legal powers except perhaps very infrequently as an ultimate sanction, and ought therefore new procedures to be devised for a more effective system of company control for, at the least, very large companies?

The failure to produce new systems of control arises partly because it is easier to diagnose what is wrong with the existing system than to find an alternative method of accountability capable of the precision and enforceability needed for embodiment in law. More importantly, reform has lacked urgency as long as the limited liability company, despite the unreality of shareholder control, continued to be a broadly successful vehicle for technological innovation and economic growth. The fact that the present system has worked, albeit imperfectly, and that other forms of ownership and control which have so far been tried in this country, for example nationalization, have not been

[1] See, e.g., *Britain's Industrial Future*, by the Industrial Enquiry Committee, Liberal Party, published by Ernest Benn, 1928; and A. A. Berle and Gardiner Means, *The Modern Corporation and Private Property*, Macmillan, 1932.

11

conspicuously successful, has left the onus of proof of the superiority of new ways of making company boards accountable on those who advocate their introduction. However, though shareholder apathy is a long-recognized phenomenon, the growth of giant companies which are multiproduct and multinational was certain to revive again questions concerning the power and accountability of the men who run them, and the nature of their responsibilities to the community in which they operate.

It is widely claimed that company boards do already take into account certain social obligations which they believe it is their duty to undertake and that these self-imposed responsibilities can be a very effective part of the system of company control, although they are not prescribed by law. Indeed the commonest explanation of company board decision-making is to describe it as a balancing of interests in which the board takes into account the interests of various groups, such as employees, customers, and the general public as well as its shareholders. It is by no means clear, however, whether this is a useful explanation of company decisions, since little is known about the way these different factors are taken into account and how much weight is attached to each. PEP, with the aid of a grant from the Social Science Research Council, decided therefore to try to explore through selected case studies how company boards viewed their responsibilities and how they explained their behaviour where they appeared to be pursuing non-profit-seeking goals. It was hoped that the study would throw some light on what is currently accepted practice among leading companies and indicate whether and where there might be a need for changes in company law.

There were a number of reasons which made such an enquiry timely, not least of which was the advent of a Labour government which had announced its intention to review the responsibilities of company boards and to make proposals for more closely controlling their activities in the interests of their employees and of the general public.

While the Labour Party remained committed to the introduction of extensive public ownership they were not greatly concerned about the impotence of shareholders. They looked to nationalization as a means of organizing industry more efficiently (cutting out 'wasteful' competition, controlling basic industries and making private monopolies public); more justly (profit for private assets would not take precedence over the interests of workers); and more democratically (workers would have more direct and indirect representation in the enterprises in which they were employed). In the event, the nationalized industries have not proved conspicuously more successful than private corporations in finding new solutions for public account-ability and the harmonious representation of workers' interests, or in distinguishing what should be their non-profit-seeking activities from responsibilities which, it is objected, present company law allows private industry to ignore. However, the disenchantment of many people in the Labour Party with public ownership as a general nostrum for industrial democracy,[1] and the limited results so far achieved by changing the ownership of industry, have given fresh impetus to the search for other ways of effecting public control over private industry and of securing a more powerful representation of interests other than those of the shareholders in company policies.

Three other factors have been of especial importance in adding to the current demand for a new definition of company responsibilities, whether in practice or in law. Two are part of long-term trends, likely to persist, which are leading to the development in industry of more democratic styles of management. First, changes in the characteristics of the labour force which derive from better education, higher wages and full employment, together with a changing technology, make it seem not only possible but highly desirable to draw operatives and junior management into a more participative pattern of company organization. Secondly, the professionalization of management means that many of a company's staff derive their standards of business behaviour from the professional bodies to which they belong, and companies cannot, even if they wished to, dictate policies auto-cratically without reference to the powerful influence of these external standards. 'As management becomes more professional and as trade union officials become more sophisticated in economics, the Board can be expected to be under more and more challenge from its sub-ordinates and from those negotiating with it across the table.'[2]

The third and more immediate factor is that the lack of economic success nationally during much of the postwar period has brought the performance of business firms constantly under public scrutiny. Since their success or otherwise in output and exports is seen to be directly related to the balance of payments and other national economic problems, this gives support to the idea that companies must be subjected to such control as will make their profit-seeking congruent with the Government's overall economic strategy, and thus responsive to the needs of the community as a whole.

Although the patent divergence between law and practice in rela-tion to shareholder control is the deficiency most often seized upon by

[1] See C. A. R. Crosland, *The Future of Socialism*, Jonathan Cape, 1956.
[2] Lord Cole, *The Future of the Board*, The Industrial Education and Research Foundation, 1968.

company law reformers it is not only this lack of accountability with which public debate is concerned. The internal government of companies, the ways in which the interests of other groups such as employees, customers and creditors as well as those of shareholders are balanced, and the relation of companies with the communities in which they operate, are all said to be in need of review and clarification, and the debate centres upon the ways in which companies can be made to recognize and serve certain social responsibilities without impairing their efficiency. From this standpoint a reform of company law which was limited to improving the flow of information to shareholders or protecting minority interests is regarded as a very limited measure rather in the nature of a first instalment; and the Companies Act of 1967 was introduced by government spokesmen as just this, with the promise of another Companies Bill to follow which would 're-examine the whole theory and purpose of the limited joint stock company, the comparative rights and obligations of shareholders, directors, creditors, employees, and the community as a whole'.[1]

POWER AND THE LARGE CORPORATION

Such a review could be addressed to a number of shortcomings in the present working of incorporated companies, but it will certainly have to deal with two principal objections which are very frequently raised. The first is that boards of large companies exercise power without effective accountability, and thus individuals and business oligarchies are said to perpetuate their grasp of office, wielding largely uncontrolled power over the fortunes of their companies and the livelihoods of their employees and, with the increasing size and interrelation of companies, over a wide area of the social and economic life of the community. That the large company should become the repository of such power is a trend which is said to be an inevitable and irreversible consequence of modern technology. Buttressed by massive advertising and research and run by professional managers and technicians, the large corporation in conditions of monopoly and near monopoly does not respond, it is said, to public demand but itself determines what products and prices it will impose upon the hapless consumer.[2] Further, since an organized and informed demand from the owners for the highest return on their investment is lacking, the boards of such companies are under no pressure to drive for maximum efficiency. Depending on the competitiveness of their environment, top executives, who are the only true insiders with

[1] President of the Board of Trade, *Hansard*, 14 February 1967.
[2] See J. K. Galbraith, *The New Industrial State*, Hamish Hamilton, 1967.

exclusive knowledge of the real state of their company's affairs, may settle for a quiet life by buying off union demands, or may seek their own advancement by promoting the company's over-rapid expansion, or may pursue any one of a number of policies not primarily directed towards an optimum return to the shareholders. Directors are said to admit privately that their dividend decision is the answer to the question 'What is the least we can get away with giving to the shareholders?' Most companies, it appears, do not need the blessing of a government policy of dividend restraint or fiscal measures to incline them to want to plough back surpluses rather than distribute them; and the more they can resort to self-financing the less they are subject to any discipline from the risk or loan capital markets.

Such arguments about the unbridled power of company boards tend to be overstated for a number of reasons[1] not the least of which is the existence of effective though imperfect[2] competition in substantial sectors of industry among many small and medium-sized firms. Even very large companies in conditions of oligopoly or duopoly may still be subject to sharp competition (as, for example, Unilever and Proctor & Gamble) in some, if not all sectors of their business, and other large international companies frequently have foreign if not domestic competition. The clash of battle between giant companies has not been uncommon in the spate of takeovers and mergers which have convulsed British boardrooms in the last ten years and which have demonstrated that companies underutilizing their resources, almost however large, cannot insulate themselves from the competition of enterprises which can make a more attractive offer to their shareholders. Nor does their power protect them from the uncertainties of the market place; large companies can be found among those with very uneven profit records. If it is the lack of competition which encourages the sovereign power of companies the remedy may lie in checking the development of monopolies and reversing any government policies which prove counter productive to a competitive environment for enterprise. In fact, the powers of government departments directly to refer companies or whole industries to agencies like the Monopolies Commission or the Prices and Incomes Board, together with the explicit assumption by governments of responsibilities to take major economic decisions, already severely limit the autonomy of business decisions.

As for social responsibility, the larger the company the less likely it is to be able to use its power unobtrusively and the more likely to be

[1] See, e.g., G. C. Allen, *Economic Fact and Fantasy*, Institute of Economic Affairs, 1967.

[2] Imperfect in the sense of the textbook model.

exposed to public comment and to be sensitive to public opinion. Big companies are not often found lagging seriously behind the average provision of fringe benefits, industrial training, support for charities and education and the preservation of public amenities, though proportionately they are often not as generous as some smaller companies.[1]

There are other constraints which limit the autocracy of company boards. Industrial and social legislation imposes responsibilities concerning matters like health, safety, training and continuity of employment, and organized labour in conditions of full employment is powerful in sustaining the worker's interests against competing claims. There are also limits which are imposed on and accepted by businessmen themselves, the breach of which may carry powerful sanctions, such as Stock Exchange rules, takeover codes, and agreements effected through employers' associations.

From their seats on the board, the businessmen whom we interviewed did not see themselves as wielding autocratic power. They are more likely to feel that they and their colleagues have only a very restricted field in which to manoeuvre for advantage between the constraints of law, the power of organized labour, the challenge of competitors and the pressure to conform to government policy. In fact, boards often feel impaled upon a kind of Morton's Fork. If they are too narrowly concerned with profit-seeking they are condemned as lacking in awareness of their social obligations; if they exercise influence beyond their boardrooms they are said to be too powerful.

The checks and restraints upon corporate power noted above suggest that the power of the modern technostructure which Galbraith has called the 'mature corporation' is probably exercised within a much narrower range of discretion than he and others suppose. Yet it cannot be disputed that company boards, at any rate in large companies with dispersed shareholdings, do exercise power without any direct and close accountability in between the ritual dance of annual meetings.

The view that large companies have too much power is often countered, of course, by the objection that they are already too greatly restricted by regulations and controls, and whether companies are thought to have too much power or too much regulation, or possibly both, depends upon the criteria by which they are judged. Are they organizations concerned primarily with profit-seeking activities which exist to produce goods and services the public wants at a price the public is willing to pay? If so, it may be possible to achieve this only by allowing boards complete discretion to make decisions and act

[1] See p. 113.

16

upon them. The voting rights of shareholders are then quite properly only a reserve power and certainly not to be used to intervene in the day-to-day management of the company's affairs; moreover, this is not inconsistent with democratic shareholder control. Company boards are not, of course, the only bodies open to the charge of being self-perpetuating oligarchies. There are many examples of organizations which are not accountable to any constituency except in a way as tenuous and indirect as that of most company boards to their shareholders. Office holders in foundations and learned societies, universities and other public and voluntary bodies often provide competent government of their affairs without its being in any real sense self-government. Whether industrial democracy ought to be embodied in company organization depends upon the view held of the corporate function. Is a large company a kind of private government which exercises such power over its members that it needs to be made subject to some kind of constitutional laws which set out clearly the rights and duties of all parties involved in the company's activities? Is the impact of these activities on the community such as to require that consideration of the public interest must often take precedence over profit-seeking, and if so, can the circumstances in which this requirement is to operate be clearly and predictably identified so that companies may be in no doubt as to where their responsibilities lie?

COMPANY SIZE

Demand for a more effective system of company control usually arises from concern about very large companies, especially the giant international corporations, but the great majority of companies are of such varying size and structure that proposals directed towards very large companies may be quite inappropriate for the thousands of much smaller ones. The idea that company law should recognize certain types of companies as being so different as to entitle them to different treatment was formerly recognized in the status of exempt private companies (abolished in the Companies Act 1967). Leading professional accountancy bodies have recently made a plea for a new classification to distinguish between what they term a 'proprietary' company whose management also owns control of it and a 'stewardship' company whose owners leave its management to an appointed board.[1] Classification as a proprietary company, it is suggested, would be subject to limits on turnover, numbers of members and of

[1] *Companies Legislation in the 1970s*, The Institutes of Chartered Accountants in England and Wales, Scotland and Ireland, and the Association of Certified and Corporate Accountants, 1969.

employees and a prohibition on offering shares to the public, and
would thus cover the smaller companies which are substantially owned
and controlled by the same people. This would take into account the
fact that though there are about half a million companies registered,
97 per cent are private companies. Even among the much smaller
number actually trading (some 288,000 companies assessed for tax in
1968), 90 per cent had incomes of less than £10,000[1] and about two-
thirds were close companies under the direct control of their owners.

Numbers (approximate) of companies by size of net income

No. of companies	Net income not exceeding £	Percentage of all companies trading
260,000	10,000	90.3
21,700	10–100,000	7.5
2,350	100–500,000	.8
4,000	over 500,000	1.4
288,000		100.0

Thus of the 28,000 companies with more than £10,000 income,
over 24,000 (85 per cent) have less than half a million pounds net
income, and the remainder, which are broadly the 4,000 companies
quoted on the stock exchange (though there are some large unquoted
companies), may have anything from £1 million to £20 million or
more net income. Among the leading 500 companies,[2] which range
by size of capital employed from £7 million and to over £150 million,
only twenty-five had over £20 million net profits (1968). Of course the
very great size of the really big companies and the share they control
of total assets in their industries make them important, irrespective
of their small numbers, but when proposals are made for reforming
company law it should be remembered how untypical at present these
few giant corporations are of industrial organization as a whole in
Britain.[3] It is true that this picture may be changing rapidly. A recent
report of the Monopolies Commission[4] has provided figures to show
that the number of quoted companies acquired by large companies

[1] *Companies Legislation in the 1970s*, The Institutes of Chartered Accountants
in England and Wales, Scotland and Ireland, and the Association of Certified and
Corporate Accountants, 1969.

[2] *The First 500 Companies*, The Times Index, 1968–9.

[3] For a fuller discussion of the need for different legal treatment for companies
of differing sizes see Tom Hadden, *The Control of Company Fraud*, PEP Broadsheet 503, 1968.

[4] *Report on the Proposed Acquisition of the De La Rue Company by the Rank
Organisation*, General Observations on Mergers, House of Commons Paper 298,
HMSO, June 1969.

was twice as great (140) in 1968 as in 1964, and the number of quoted companies with net assets of over £500,000 fell by a third between 1961 and 1968. In a survey of 1,312 companies of this size (i.e. over £500,000 assets) twenty-eight of the largest companies held 50 per cent of total net assets in 1968 as against 39 per cent in 1961, and in 1967 the net assets of the 100 largest companies were nearly 60 per cent of the total in manufacturing industry compared with 55 per cent in 1963. In certain industrial groups the degree of concentration was even greater.

However, these large companies are not so powerful that they are easily able, as Galbraith and others have suggested, to maintain high profits steadily. Some very large companies are to be found among those with a steady profit growth, others have a very erratic record and some have persistently declined. There is little evidence that size as such leads to efficiency. By the measure of return on capital employed, less than 10 per cent of the first 100 largest companies[1] had more than 20 per cent return, compared with one-fifth among those ranked between 400th and 500th in size; while among companies much too small to rate a place in the first 500 British companies many earn a substantially higher return on their assets than some of the giants. The companies which appear in the Top Ten in Britain judged by growth and by profitability are, with notable exceptions (Tesco, Beecham, etc.), rarely found among the 100 largest companies; and countries which have smaller average plant sizes than Britain, e.g. France, Japan and Italy, have not been thereby prevented from showing a record of success. The substitution of parent or holding company control for shareholder control in large enterprises does not automatically put them in a position to command the kind of economic success[2] which might be expected from their size and market power.

The very largest companies are not as large as the nationalized industries but it has been suggested that they most closely resemble public corporations, both being managed by much the same sort of people for much the same sort of ends. The problems of public and large private corporations in establishing effective supervision of their professional managers and a satisfactory relationship with their owners are held to be very similar, and have led to the argument that one enterprise or corporation law ought to be devised to be suitable for both.[3] Certainly the very great disparity in size among companies

---

[1] *The First 500 Companies*, The Times Index, 1968–9.
[2] C. F. Pratten, 'The Merger Boom in the Manufacturing Industry', *Lloyds Bank Review*, October 1968.
[3] M. Fogarty, *Company and Corporation, One Law?* Geo. Chapman, 1965.

suggests that there must be difficulties in devising any one form of company control which can be at once appropriate for the giant company and the small retailer.

THE PARAMOUNTCY OF SHAREHOLDER INTERESTS

The second major objection to existing company law and practice is the narrowness of its concern with the shareholders' interests; that is, even if the shareholders' interests were truly treated as of paramount concern by company boards, this is not to be considered satisfactory. Thus, where control is in the hands of a few shareholders, often family-related, the criticism of these companies is not the lack of accountability but its narrowness. The complaint here is that the shareholders' interest is only one of a number of interests served by the company and should not automatically take precedence over all other interests such as those of employees, customers, creditors and the general public. This 'balance of interests' concept of board responsibilities has been widely quoted by such diverse authorities as the late Editor of the *Investors' Chronicle*, the Institute of Directors, and a Socialist President of the Board of Trade. It is moreover generally accepted by many company boards themselves. But when directors who were interviewed[1] were asked to explain what the term meant, beyond the simple proposition that directors when making decisions should take account of all the parties and factors they know to be involved, there was no clear answer. Indeed, the possible implication that boards have indefinite and all-embracing responsibilities worried some of the directors, who said that the concept, if taken really seriously by company boards, might lead to their aggrandizement rather than to public accountability—if it did not at the same time lead to their paralysis. As far as the company law is concerned, it was pointed out that such a concept cannot be offered as a substitute for a clear and legally enforceable definition of the duties and responsibilities of company boards.

There are two main propositions to which the balance-of-interests concept of company duties usually leads: one is that boards have social responsibilities involving non-profit-seeking activities or activities in which profit is moderated for some socially useful purpose; the other (which is consistent with the first but is often put forward by different people), is that, since companies should study the interests of their employees and do so in a socially acceptable, i.e. democratic way, the workers ought to have formal rights to influence, participate in, or control (the proposals vary) the conduct of the company's

---

[1] See p. 23 *et seq.*

business, including the way in which profit is shared. It was with such aspects of companies' social responsibilities (which are seen by some as the basis of a code of company conduct and by some as provisions to be written into the company law) that the PEP study was concerned. Company boards were asked what they thought social responsibility meant in the context of business decisions, and how they saw themselves as fulfilling the requirement that they be socially responsible. Did they see this as representing a beneficent change of corporate purpose in which company boards would moderate the pursuit of profit, to the benefit of other considerations? Or were they hesitant about accepting this invitation to increase their already considerable powers by using the companies' resources to effect the social ends particular businessmen think desirable? The case studies, reported in Chapters 2 to 5, were also designed to throw light on these questions.

Chapter 1

Company Boards and their Social Responsibilities

The idea that business companies should try to act in a socially responsible way is now so widely accepted that it is rare to hear any view expressed to the contrary. Even those who stoutly defend industry's primary duty to make profits agree that these are to be pursued in a socially responsible way, by which they usually mean within the context of a generous concern for the well-being of their employees and a due regard for the 'public interest'. The reasons for the nearly unanimous acceptance of these ideas are not far to seek. Governments who are seeking further control of economic activity find useful support for their interventionist policies in directing industry in the national interest. Unions can press their claims on the grounds that companies ought to put the human needs of labour before profits. Economists concerned with the theory of the firm who can see no other way of legitimizing the power of large corporations and quasi-monopolies may agree that, as long as a secure level of earnings and provision for reinvestment are maintained, some part of the company's resources should be diverted to purposes broadly useful to the community as a whole. Sociologists explain the images businessmen have of themselves as socially responsible in terms of psychological 'fields' which attract people towards what are currently the most highly valued goals, and thus corporate image making is turned into a new kind of business idealism rather than an advertising gimmick.[1] The teachers of business management are glad to have some rationale by which to explain to their students observable business behaviour which clearly is not profit-maximizing, and which may improve the esteem society accords to the occupation their pupils are about to enter. All these factors both influence and are influenced by the idea that business companies have other duties than simply those which serve exclusively the interests of their shareholders or

[1] See George S. Odiorne, 'The Great Image Hunt', *Michigan Business Review*, January 1966; and M. Fogarty, *Wider Business Objectives*, PEP Broadsheet No. 495, May 1966.

even those of the company's own employees; all provide powerful support for the idea that industry has wider responsibilities which must not be neglected in the pursuit of profits.

Clearly, if the rule of social responsibility were applied to every business decision, a board's responsibilities would be extended far beyond its own company. 'Industrial relations can no longer be treated as a private matter between employers and unions. Both sides of industry have a responsibility not just to shareholders and their members but to the community as a whole'.[1] This statement expresses a general view, and no less a representative of business opinion than the former Director of the Confederation of British Industry has stated that 'the right to make decisions with consideration solely for the individual enterprise can hardly be sustained'.[2]

COMPANY RESPONSIBILITIES AS DEFINED BY LARGE COMPANIES

To gain some insight into the way businessmen at board level themselves interpret their corporate responsibilities, the views were sought of the chairman or managing director of twenty-five large companies (twenty of them were in the first 100 companies ranked by capital employed).[3] Only large companies were included in the study because size seemed to be most frequently linked in the minds both of company critics and company boards themselves with the idea of some special kind of responsibility arising from the exercise of considerable economic power. The companies were selected at random and included firms engaged in brewing, construction, rubber, paper, textiles, food, aircraft engines, electrical engineering, tobacco, cement, sugar and oil refining, and in retail trade: fifteen produced branded goods which retailed directly to the public. Interviews, to outline the objects of the enquiry, were sought first with the chairman or managing director, and in eighteen of the companies approached, one or other discussed what they conceived to be the functions and responsibilities of their boards. In six companies the interviews were given by other senior board members (two of them company secretaries), and in one case all the enquiries were handled through a Trade and Public Relations Department. (In this company, however, a great deal of information was already available in printed form, and the heads of six departments answered questions.) After experimentation

---

[1] *The Observer*, May 25, 1969.
[2] John Davies, on Industry and Government, *Sir George Earle Memorial Lecture*, published by Industrial Educational and Research Foundation, 1966.
[3] *The First 500 Companies*, The Times Index, 1968–9.

in three companies who responded, over a period of several months, to a range of questions, a list of questions was drawn up designed to ascertain what general employment and welfare policies companies were pursuing and how they related these to their concepts of their responsibilities to employees and to the community. Fifteen companies agreed to answer these questions, and gave a number of interviews in the course of which non-board-members, such as personnel directors, economists and company secretaries, were brought into the discussions. The statements of company spokesmen were checked against the actual behaviour of their company, e.g. only those companies which gave details of actual circumstances in which they had moderated profit in deference to 'public interest' were recorded as being likely to practise this kind of restraint.

All of the company representatives accepted the general idea that companies should act in a socially responsible way, and all but one described their activities in terms of a service to the public. Only one managing director said uncompromisingly that the object of the company was to make money. The respondents in these companies conceived their social responsibilities as lying in two main directions: in their relations with their employees, and in their impact on the community in which they were located. In industrial relations a company's record in the provision of security of employment, safe working conditions, fringe benefits and a general concern for the well-being of employees were the main criteria, with a minority of company boards also emphasizing joint consultative procedures. In public relations, responsible corporate citizenship was measured by the companies themselves according to readiness to make company donations to charities and the arts, to take part in public affairs, and to protect public amenities from industrial damage. The company whose managing director said that profit was his organization's prime objective had been as active as other companies in pioneering employee welfare, but he regarded this simply as intelligent management. On the other hand, donations to charitable bodies he considered inappropriate as a corporate function and his company's contributions were reluctant and restricted to those objects which had some definite business pay-off for the company.

Figures I and II indicate the actual performance of the fifteen companies consulted on specified areas of industrial and community relations—and in which they had taken the initiative in developing policies. From this it will be seen that in this group, acting in a socially responsible way was primarily interpreted as being a good employer, with an interest in public affairs which could be underwritten from time to time from the company's funds. In industrial

FIGURE I: *Profile of fifteen companies by their employment policies*

Employment Policies	Number of Companies
	1 2 3 4 5 6 7 8 9 10 11 12 13 14 15
Company initiated and carried out regular wage reviews i.e. did not wait for wage claims	
Encouraged union membership Facilitated work of union representatives	
Expected to give leadership in industrial relations in their industry	
Put maintaining security of employment as principal company objective	
Accepted fully obligations for training and retraining employees	
Had provided benefits, e.g. pensions, before and beyond statutory schemes	
Paid special attention to safety in working conditions	
Had joint consultative production committees regularly meeting	
Had provided sick pay and redundancy pay before and beyond statutory schemes	
Was prepared on occasion to keep employees beyond usefulness to the company	
Had improved status of hourly paid employees by 'key' and 'star' schemes etc.	
Schemes for staff status for all employees under discussion	
Used prior consultation with employees before new working rules introduced	
Used joint committee for the management of fringe benefits, e.g. pension funds	
Offered favourable terms for employee shareholding	
Used prior consultation with employees before introducing new fringe benefits	
Encouraged employee shareholding (but without special concessions)	
Had profit sharing scheme	
Had prior consultation with staff before declaring redundancy	

25

FIGURE II: *Profile of fifteen companies by their response to community needs*

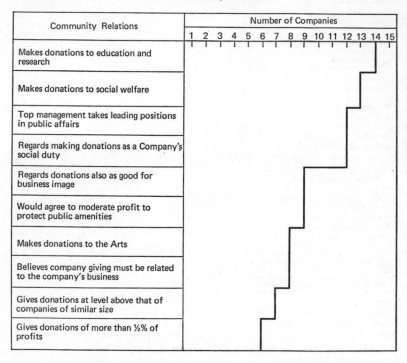

relations about three-quarters of the company respondents thought that having a positive employment policy which recognized the needs of workers for security of employment, and in which regular wage reviews were initiated (rather than waiting for wage demands), was the best procedure. This it was thought could be done only by recognizing and working with strong union organizations. The introduction of fringe benefits like redundancy pay and sick benefits in advance of any legal requirement to do so[1] was characteristic of about half of the group, and in three-quarters of the companies there was an active concern for safety and well-organized training and retraining schemes for employees. A small minority of the companies wanted to improve the status of hourly-paid employees, to encourage

[1] The questions distinguished between innovation in industrial welfare, and merely keeping up with other companies as a matter of prestige and labour recruitment, etc.

them to become shareholders and to bring them into a profit-sharing scheme. The great majority had systems of joint consultation for the discussion of production problems, but there was a very limited use of prior consultation in matters of redundancy or before introducing new welfare schemes. Managements to date had retained the initiative in such decisions as declaring redundancies or devising severance pay schemes, though the administration of these decisions once made was generally a matter for consultation.[1]

In a company's relations with the community, generous donations, the acceptance by industrialists of public office, and a concern for the preservation of public amenities were considered important by the majority of the companies studied. But though boards interpreted connections with the company's business very broadly for the purpose of making donations, they were on the whole content with giving what was expected from companies of their size, and they all spoke of exercising great care in what they described as 'giving away the shareholders' money'.

All companies agreed that they would expect to pursue their business ends with due regard for the public interest and that this would mean from time to time accepting legislative restraints which they considered inimical to their interests. They were less reconciled to the idea of having to adapt (some said distort), their business decisions to accord with the government's general economic policy, but none thought that objections should be carried to the point of confrontation with government by total refusal to co-operate. Quite apart from other ways in which the government could vent its displeasure on uncooperative companies, for a number of companies in this group the government was one, if not the largest, of their customers.

RATIONALE FOR NON-PROFIT-SEEKING ACTIVITIES OF COMPANIES

Company respondents claimed to do these things for two main reasons: first, because it was expedient, i.e. they believed it to be good for their business; and secondly, because they genuinely believed these activities to be worth while and part of their responsibilities and preferred to moderate profit in order to finance them. In the first case they may believe that a particular activity will yield a specific business return, e.g. pleasing an important customer, or that sponsoring higher education and research will be indirectly advantageous because

[1] This enquiry was made in 1966 and would not probably be typical of the amount of productivity bargaining now taking place.

the supply of trained personnel needed for their industry will be increased. They may also believe that they are behaving in the way which is expected of them in the social environment in which they have to operate, and of which they and their employees are a part. They do this because they judge that profitable business activity will be acceptable and unhampered only if it is accompanied by behaviour that is held to be responsible. On this explanation, generous fringe benefits, provision for redundant employees, corporative charity, honest dealing with consumers, etc. etc., are a form of sophisticated public relations, which satisfies the expectations of the community including the company's employees and customers, and which is not inconsistent with, and perhaps is necessary for, maximizing profit in the long run. This type of responsible company activity is often seen most clearly where companies have operated in other than a domestic market. British companies which have operated overseas and built schools and hospitals and provided other services are familiar with the need to make themselves 'acceptable' as a necessary business objective. If this is the explanation of some non-profit-making activity—viz. companies are responding to what is expected of them in terms of the values and mores of the society in which they operate —a calculating attitude to philanthropy will, if apparent, defeat the company's purpose. Its contribution to community life may not enhance its reputation if it is judged to be cynical and self-seeking.[1] Further, it can be argued that if a company innovates in a non-profit-making activity for business reasons, it will have to risk the fact that its competitors may quickly copy its programme so that the company will lose its business advantage as an innovator; and once having established these non-profit-making expenditures it cannot reduce them even if they no longer serve a business purpose.

Where behaviour that is accepted as being socially responsible is also reckoned to be profitable for shareholders in the long run, no problem is raised in relation to existing company law. But some directors believe they have a positive duty to pursue socially responsible policies even if it is at the expense of the shareholder's long-run profit.

How much of this non-profit-seeking activity a company can undertake might be expected to depend in part on how competitive its

---

[1] The alleged use of foundations for tax avoidance and company control by some American corporations was the basis from which it was successfully argued that new restrictions should be placed upon the operation of company foundations (see pp. 104–105 below). The reputation of the foundations for enlightened and genuinely charitable activities has been seriously blemished by the apparent cynicism of their sponsors.

business setting is, and in part on the degree of control exerted (perhaps through extensive shareholding) by one or a few members of a board who genuinely believe in philanthropy and like to have a reputation for being progressive employers.

Such explanations do not seem to account for the many cases of companies in highly competitive industries which nevertheless allocate resources to non-profit-making activities, especially those which actually innovate in philanthropic contributions or in employee welfare. Nor do they explain why some companies with an indifferent profit record and widely dispersed shareholdings are generous above the average in non-profit-seeking expenditures.

CASE STUDIES OF COMPANIES EXERCISING WHAT THEY BELIEVE ARE THEIR SOCIAL RESPONSIBILITIES

From further enquiries among company boards it seemed that the concept of company responsibilities described by the fifteen companies consulted were typical of widely-held views, and three aspects of these company policies were, therefore, selected for closer examination. Case studies were made in two areas of what appeared to be non-profit-seeking business activities, and in two situations where companies were trying or being pressed to try to take greater account of the interests of employees and customers. These were:

1. A study of job security involving the attempts of one company to offer continuity of employment in a chronically casual industry.

2. A study of four companies' donative policies and the rationales offered by them and by a much larger group of companies (eighty-two) for devoting company resources to non-profit-seeking activities.

3. A study of a company's response to a government request to reduce the prices of its products on the grounds that the proportion of costs arising from selling and promotion expenses was excessive and therefore against consumers' interests.

4. A study of the development of a more democratic system of company organization in which a very large company has attempted to work towards explicit company objectives through a participative style of management.

This shows the subjects in descending order of general acceptance by boards as to what social responsibility means, viz. good employment practices, company gifts, and deferring to the public interest. Although the subject of the fourth study is likely to make much more difference in the long run as to how responsibilities are interpreted, because it is a change in institutions and practice, this did not spring to people's minds and had a low rating in the thinking of those interviewed.

This last study of an exercise in a style of management involving a greater degree of participation by employees arose less directly than the others from the generally expressed views of company boards who believed they were sensitive to their social responsibilities. While boards accepted that they had to be concerned with the interests of their employees, they were not prepared for employees to be put in a position in the company from which they could advance their own interests on equal terms with management and shareholders. Yet the idea that boards should in some way balance the interests of a number of groups, among whom workers would be prominent, was a sufficiently attractive one to some companies to encourage them to experiment with devising company objectives which could be agreed by employees as well as management, and by involving employees directly in some aspects of company decision making.

Chapter 2

Case Study I: Participative Management

Direct representation of workers on the boards of companies in the private sector of industry has not yet been accepted in Britain, although worker directors in an advisory capacity have been appointed to the British Steel Corporation. Full workers' control of industrial enterprises remains a 'misty millennium' for most people—including most workers' representatives—but if the composition of company boards were to be subject to new legal requirements, such as the creation of supervisory boards as in Germany, it is very likely that employees' representatives would be included in them. On the other hand, more effective representation of employees' interests in the day-to-day management of industry is an immediate practical objective. Though this may be viewed by companies primarily as a better technique of management, provision for consultation and opportunities for junior management and operatives to have more control over working arrangements could in fact not only change the quality of management–employee relationships but also the distribution of power.

The case for more participation by workers and their representatives in the management of the enterprise in which they are employed is now widely accepted, but the diversity of views about how this can best be implemented reflects in part the very different purposes of the different interests involved.

Some forms of what might be called participation, of course, already exist widely in industry, and have done for many years, though in general, only a very limited and ineffectual use is made of the machinery which exists. In many companies there are bodies variously called joint committees, works councils, etc., on which nominees of management sit with representatives[1] of employees and engage in some form of communication and consultation about workshop and

[1] Some of these are heirs of works councils and joint production committees set up during the last war; others have a much longer history in companies which have always taken the view that their employees have a right to be consulted about certain aspects of company policy which most directly affect them.

plant problems other than those which are reserved for union–management negotiation. Outside such formal procedure for joint consultation or collective bargaining, employees' representatives have other ways of powerfully influencing the conduct of a company's business. The decisions of management which, without prior consultation, are imposed upon their employees are paralleled by the unilateral decisions which workers and their representatives imposed upon management, e.g. restrictive practices, overtime bans, etc. A participative form of management seeks to reduce the exercise by both sides of this kind of power and to widen instead the areas of agreed joint action.

The need for an increase in the participation of workers in management is argued on two main grounds.

First, that as a matter of social justice, workers have a right to take part in the decisions of the company in which they work and on which their livelihood depends, in order to protect their legitimate interests. To do this they must be represented at all levels of decision-making in the company and have access to the kind of information they need to do business with the company as sellers of labour.

Secondly, that workers have a contribution to make which will increase the efficiency of the enterprise. There are untapped reserves of skill and experience which can be harnessed to the company's efforts if workers are consulted and given responsibility. The exercise of this responsibility it is believed will develop their capacity to add both to the company's productive output and to their own job satisfactions. Thus gaining the co-operation of employees at all levels by enabling them to understand and participate in company decisions is at once a more democratic and a more effective way of managing an enterprise than an authoritarian style of management. On this view, joint management–worker groups function as production committees seeking the most efficient methods of operating the plant. A major factor in this will be dealing with workers' dissatisfactions which if not removed will seriously impede progress.

These approaches overlap to some extent: both involve giving employees more information about their company's objectives, consulting them about the implementation of company policy, and extending their responsibilities and control over their own jobs. In practice, attempts to implement these general intentions reveal a considerable gulf between those who, in seeking greater influence and control for workers in the general conduct of the company's business, are in effect asking for co-determination, and those on the management side who are looking for a more acceptable and effective style of management but who are not prepared to go far beyond joint consultation. Both approaches involve increased *direct* participation, i.e. by individual employees, and *indirect* participation, i.e. by representatives of workers, in company management. Where the rights of workers as an interest group are the paramount consideration, however, emphasis tends to be placed upon representative participation at all levels, including the board, where major company decisions are made, and in all matters, not simply in decisions directly related to employment policies. Where the emphasis is on seeking greater efficiency by obtaining a more co-operative and informed contribution from employees, on the other hand, managements try to enlarge the direct participation of individual employees in the decisions which control the detailed daily organization of their jobs, rather than relying only on consultation and negotiation with workers' representatives. This latter approach is not necessarily motivated by a desire to by-pass the representative machinery but can arise from experiences in which this machinery has proved to be ineffective, either because it did not command any real interest or support (e.g. moribund works councils), or because it became a source of unresolved conflicts.

The direct participation of workers in the ownership of their companies by employee shareholdings is not very widespread in British industry. There is nothing to prevent individuals (or unions) from buying ordinary shares and with them a shareholder's rights to information and to vote, though, clearly, schemes which allot shares as a form of profit-sharing or offer them to employees on favourable terms give a more positive encouragement to share-ownership. There are, however, some important objections to profit-sharing and employee shareholding schemes which limit enthusiasm for them among trade-unionists and even among some employers who are in other respects leaders in providing extra-statutory benefits for their employees.

Yet if power in a company derives from ownership, one way of bringing workers' interests into the power structure of a company could be to give them special encouragement to acquire shares and in this way some influence over its direction. Employee shareholding is closely linked to profit-sharing, because the majority of schemes provide participation in profits through the offer of shares, often with qualifications attached to their disposal.

The optional benevolent type of profit-sharing schemes are not designed to give workers anything approaching real influence in the companies concerned. In so far as employers who operate schemes have articulated their motives[1] at all, they believe that profit-sharing

[1] Guy Naylor, *Sharing the Profits*, Garnstone Press, 1968, p. 106.

33

schemes, in addition to their wider social value of encouraging savings and providing for retirement, serve to create greater interest in and identification with the company, and to provide incentives. Even the most enthusiastic companies, however, agree that the effects are very limited, especially among junior staff and operatives. The evidence on how long shares are kept is confused, depending in part on the conditions attached to their issue and the eligibility requirements for employees, but almost certainly a substantial amount are encashed at the earliest opportunity.

Employers interviewed during this study who were not willing to introduce schemes argued that it is not the business of a company to reward its employees in a form which is not immediately negotiable and which also influences them to risk their savings as well as their working career in the same company. Nor do they believe it should be in amounts which might vary annually in a way which individual employees may have little chance to influence directly. Trade-unionists are generally doubtful whether profit-sharing schemes have much influence on either incentives or improved labour relations. To the extent that the shares or cash are a bonus from employers not negotiated by the unions the latter's influence may be weakened (all company-initiated fringe benefits suffer from this disadvantage in the eyes of union representatives), and shareholding especially seems to be linked to the embourgeoisement of the workers.

Whatever the intentions, simple schemes tend to become complicated and this makes them unattractive to some employees. Companies find themselves having to impose limits on the size of the bonus, on the number of shares issued, and the period during which shares must be kept and this leads inevitably to complicated rules. In profit-sharing schemes, as in some pension funds and other fringe benefits, if schemes are to be fair and well founded they have to have detailed regulations, and most employees have neither the time nor the inclination to study them. Workers, it must be remembered, like shareholders, when new procedures for their involvement in company activities are devised, do not in general want to attend many meetings or wrestle with small print.

Much more far-reaching proposals than these limited profit-sharing schemes have been proposed elsewhere, e.g. in France where participation, including profit-sharing and employee shareholding, was a central plank of Gaullist labour policies, though without much result, at least as yet. The Vallon Amendment in France (1965),[1] for example, proposed that where a company reinvested part of its profits

---

[1] See also the Loichot Plan for pan-capitalism, M. Fogarty, *A Companies Act 1970?* PEP Broadsheet No. 500, 1967.

the workers should have a claim against this increase in assets. The Mathey Commission which was set up to explore the ways of making such a proposal effective, and which recommended a flexible voluntary system, emphasized the very great difficulties of making such schemes work equitably as between different groups of workers (a problem in all such schemes if made compulsory), and noted that anyway the businesses with the highest rate of self-financing paid the highest wages so the practice of increasing assets by self-financing was not hostile to the interests of employees. The committee recommended a flexible voluntary system, but a profit-sharing scheme was eventually introduced by law in 1967. Under this scheme, after tax (corporate or personal) is paid and a 5 per cent return on capital allowed, and a formula applied to adjust for the ratio of capital to labour (or otherwise workers in capital-intensive industries would be unfairly favoured), the resulting amount is divided between shareholders and employees. As the employees' share is tax-free and the employer is entitled to tax relief on the amounts paid to the employees and a part of the shareholders' share which is reinvested is also deductible from pretax profits, the net effect is simply that the cost of the scheme is largely borne by the taxpayer.

In Britain on the employers' side there are doubts about the justification of any very extensive share distribution to employees, and to this are added anxieties about the practical effects (e.g. the inflationary effects on share capital), perplexities about how to devise an equitable scheme, and reservations about the wisdom of making more than a very limited part of employees' remuneration dependent upon a residual. On the other hand, doubts expressed about how far profit-sharing schemes, in identifying the employee with the company's fortunes, are an important incentive to performance seem to be confined to operatives, and quite opposite arguments are frequently advanced for handsome stock options for executives. A good deal more research is needed on the reactions of manual workers to offers of shareholding and profit-sharing from the point of view of their impact on industrial relations and incentives, since the affluent worker may be developing different patterns of saving in which shareholding may come to play a more important part. So far it can only be said that profit-sharing and share-distribution schemes appear in most companies to follow rather than precede good industrial relations, nor is there any evidence that they are successful, in isolation, in markedly increasing employees' sense of participation in their company. Companies which are enthusiastic advocates of profit-sharing do of course, as noted earlier, believe their schemes are of value to the community by encouraging savings in general and by the small investor in particular, in addition to benefiting their employees directly, and some of the employers we interviewed regarded it as part of a company's social responsibilities to foster employee savings.

The forms of participation which are more positively canvassed in Britain are those which would give the workers and their representatives a more influential voice in the management of the plants in which they work. The three major functions in which workers' representatives might expect to play a part are in policy-making, in major executive decisions and in day-to-day management. In British companies (it would be different in countries which use two-tier boards) this would mean workers' representative(s) on the board, a works council or production committee of some kind composed jointly of management and employees in the factory, and ready access directly or through shop stewards to supervisors and line management on the shop floor. At this last level, participation could be directly experienced by the workers concerned, but at the other levels it would be implemented indirectly through their representatives. Alongside this internal structure of representation and linked directly through shop stewards are officials of the trade unions. Some of the problems of participation are at once apparent. If the system works successfully 'internally' the influence of union officials may be reduced. If on the other hand union officials are the only channel for the negotiation of important matters of wage and working conditions, how can the joint consultative machinery have any real significance for either management or men? The history of joint consultative machinery is not encouraging. Even in Glacier Metals, which pushed joint consultation much further than most, it was found that consultation by itself makes little impact on the basic attitudes of the ordinary worker; and changes had to be made in management because 'the practice of consultation was extended in such a way as to interfere with the effective management of the factory'.[1] It is a common complaint that committees have been reduced to dealing with trivia and in some cases have simply atrophied from lack of interest and support. Machinery will not work if there is no will to use it and there will be no point in adding workers' apathy to shareholders' apathy, if what is required is that both interest groups should be pressing company boards hard to justify their performance and the return yielded on both capital and labour.

The demand for representation at board level, that is a demand to share in the co-direction of the company, is not generally treated by trade unions as their most pressing claim. Some would welcome

[1] John A. Mack, 'The Glacier Metal Experiment', *Political Quarterly*, July/September, 1956.

experimentation[1] but most remain cautious, and their reasons are not far to seek. They fear that a worker's representative on the board either would tend to be ineffective, being by-passed by caucus decisions made elsewhere before board meetings, or would succumb to the pressure to become fully committed to board responsibilities and less and less a representative of a special interest group. Many trade-unionists feel that the conflict of loyalties would be irreconcilable. Professor Fogarty comments upon the German system 'the minority representation of employees on the supervisory boards of ordinary companies is perceived by employees themselves as a somewhat meaningless racket whose most notable merit is to provide a source of director's fees for deserving trade-unionists, who are elected on the basis not that they are to do an important job but that they have earned their turn at the pork barrel'.[2] Professor Fogarty has much more confidence in the German system as applied to the coal and steel industries where the representation of workers is equal to that of the shareholders and cannot therefore be overridden or absorbed so easily. The lesson seems to be that if co-determination at board level is to have any real influence on company control, there must be a substantial transfer of power to workers' representatives, which (since it is not based on any existing property rights) would have to be conferred by legislation and would carry with it unequivocally a share in responsibility for the overall direction of the company. The significance of such a move for the structure and control of companies is discussed further below (Chapter 7); here it may be noted that such representation was believed by the shop stewards with whom it was discussed to be too far removed from the shop floor to increase the sense of participation by individual workers at their place of employment. Lack of contact, lack of communication and lack of consultation were the defects they complained of in industrial relations and these workers' representatives did not think they were likely to be remedied by appointments at board level.

A works council acting as a joint consultative body at plant level seems more likely to bring representatives of management and workers into a fruitful collaboration, but this has often proved to be not the case. As long as these committees are the creatures of management and can only discuss matters referred to them, the worker members, who feel they are in a subordinate position in the hierarchy anyway,

[1] The British Steel Corporation's experiment is already in operation. Twelve Worker Directors have been appointed, though in an advisory not an executive capacity.
[2] *Worker Representation on Company Boards*, Industrial Education and Research Foundation.

37

cannot easily sustain independent criticisms of management directives about which they may have little knowledge or expertise. In these circumstances the councils are reduced to the 'state of the lavatories' level of complaints. In French and German law, works councils have status and functions laid down for them which allow them considerable influence in relation to major issues such as plans involving labour reductions, though their position is still advisory and does not conflict with the responsibility of executive management to manage. If, as is sometimes suggested, influential councils of this kind had to be elected in every plant over a certain size in Britain, what would be the relationship of these bodies and the unions, since both would claim to represent the workers? Unions are quite clear on this point, and the Labour Party's recent statement on industrial democracy[1] also settles *for single-channel bargaining.* Unions are suspicious of the creation of any bodies with duties to represent workers which are outside their influence. The problem might be overcome to some extent if union representatives are also members of all consultative committees, but this is not always so, nor are all workers members of trade unions (unions represent less than 50 per cent of the working force of the country). Here again, however, the shop stewards with whom these problems were discussed saw difficulties. They said that there are few other than the existing union representatives and the politically active who want to accept positions on works councils, and that those who do receive little support from their fellows. The evidence is indeed conflicting as to how far workers want to accept a greater degree of involvement in the organization of their work place. It can however be argued that, even if it is doubtful whether there is much interest in indirect representative responsibility, many workers would welcome greater direct involvement. This kind of participation would involve enlarged responsibility for their own jobs, readily accessible and two-way channels of communication and complaint on matters directly affecting the organization of their work, and clear and early explanations of the changes involved for them by new developments in management policies.

This democratic and participative style of management does not necessarily imply the setting up of formal representative and consultative bodies; there are other ways of seeking the understanding and co-operation of employees, especially for changed working practices, by making plain the reasons for new instructions and abandoning authoritarian management practices. This type of participation, in which a worker is involved in a specific and immediate work situation in a way which he can not merely comprehend but

[1] *Labour's Economic Strategy*, August 1969.

actively respond to and influence, was believed by managers in our case study to be capable of at least reducing tensions and frustration and at best greatly increasing job satisfaction and output. This type of participation is held to be both more genuinely democratic than a formally representative system because the way people are treated is less authoritarian, and more effective because they respond more constructively to the demands of the work situation. It has been welcomed in some quarters as the only true industrial democracy and in others dismissed as a devilish clever form of managerial manipulation of workers by which they are persuaded to commit themselves to agreed objectives but the objectives agreed turn out to be the company's objectives and are not necessarily congruent with the workers' interests.

The case study described below throws light on some of these problems, by tracing the attempt of a large international company:

(a) to establish clearly and make known to all employees agreed company objectives; and

(b) to develop a more consultative style of management, through which all employees can understand these objectives and feel able to commit themselves co-operatively to their pursuit.

THE INDUSTRY

The company is engaged in an industry which is highly capital-intensive with a relatively small labour force. One of the two plants studied here, for example, represents an investment of £50 million with operating costs of £12 million per year and employs 2,000 people. Only a highly productive labour force operating a twenty-four-hour system can make profitable use of capital outlay of these dimensions.

The industry depends largely on science for its technology and is liable to fairly rapid and frequent changes in the pattern of work due to the application of new scientific knowledge. Often the only way of making the best use of plant is by increased automation, and men in the industry are aware that from time to time the need will arise for some redeployment of labour if not actual redundancy.

The technology of the industry makes it necessary that plants are large and employees are dispersed over a wide location. This presents greater problems for establishing effective systems of communication than in plants where work is more closely concentrated and inter-related.

THE COMPANY

The industry of which this company is a leading member is one characterized by oligopolistic competition, and the company is one of a large international group. It consists of a collection of diverse affiliates with different functions which are engaged in producing, processing and distributing its products in a number of countries. The size and complexity of the group make it a target for suspicions about unlimited corporate power though in some aspects of its operations it is subject to sharp competition. The size of its assets and profits make it difficult for workers to believe that the company cannot afford to pay higher wages and grant other concessions.

Because the company is part of an international group, plant management has no direct control over raw materials, prices or markets and at times local output and profitability has to be deliberately restrained to fit in with the policies of the Group. Management has been mainly preoccupied with technical expertise in operating plant, and technical excellence has tended to be the criterion for advancement in the company. The importance of good industrial relations has not been unappreciated, but it has been difficult for management to handle labour problems firmly and fairly when under pressure to settle disputes quickly because of over-riding Group needs. Company policies, because they are part of larger Group objectives, have sometimes seemed inappropriate and contradictory at local levels and management has had difficulty in explaining their necessity to the company's employees.

THE LABOUR FORCE

The labour force, which handles expensive and potentially dangerous equipment in processes in which minor errors can have serious consequences, is divided between operators and craftsmen. The process operators, who are shift workers keeping the plant operating twenty-four hours per day, are not skilled men in the sense of being trained tradesmen and, though they perform very responsible tasks in this company, their skills would not be easily transferable outside the industry. There are nine grades of operatives whose average basic pay is just under £1,000 a year plus an average £300 shift allowance, so that their take-home pay (including overtime) is not very far behind that of the craftsmen. Foremen and supervisors are often recruited from this group. The craftsmen are mostly day workers mainly responsible for maintenance. They had been allowed to develop a regular pattern of extensive overtime working which arose from a management undertaking given in exchange for arrangements to employ extra craftsmen (or to contract work out) for special tasks during plant renewal. The craftsmen have become dependent on their premium payments as part of their regular earnings, and this makes it difficult to get any agreement to reduce overtime.

THE UNIONS

Operators are members of the Transport and General Workers Union and their stewards have on the whole been ready to co-operate with management in discussing greater job flexibility as their members are likely to gain from such developments. The craftsmen, secure in their skills and status, have been sceptical of new company proposals and through their representatives, the Joint Union Negotiating Committee, have been reluctant to be drawn into discussions for implementing the changes put forward by management. Negotiations with operatives who are members of the T&GWU used to be concluded nationally, while bargaining with craftsmen took place locally. From 1967, T&GWU negotiations have also been concluded locally and there is freedom to conclude company or plant bargains with both groups.

THE BACKGROUND

The decision to try to develop an explicit company philosophy and embody it in company objectives which could be clearly expounded and understood by all members of the company arose from concern about the unsatisfactory nature of industrial relations in the company's plants. It was felt that there was little hope of reducing overmanning and excessive overtime and of greater job flexibility and productivity bargains unless some fundamental changes could be made not only in labour relations at the one plant where these were most unsatisfactory, but in the whole style of management throughout the company. Management were conscious that they had on too many occasions failed to consult with workers and their representatives before announcing decisions affecting them and had, on the other hand, too frequently given in to pressure and allowed the establishment of payments and practices which were unnecessary and uneconomic.

Following a redundancy operation in 1964 in which the company, though making generous severance payments, had not consulted and worked with the unions as closely as they might have done, and where some residue of suspicion and uncertainty seemed likely to hinder good working relationships, an Employee Relations Planning Unit was created at Head Office. Its staff began to study how the company might move away from a conventional approach to labour relations, with its emphasis on earnings, fringe benefits and physical working

41

conditions, and try to evolve a policy which would break down barriers of mistrust between employees and management. The Unit's studies identified the basic problems of hourly-paid workers as distrust of management, lack of security, lack of status, conflicts arising from union loyalties, and a wages structure which encouraged ineffective work spread out to involve excessive overtime. Single (staff) status, annual salaries, job flexibility and a reduction in the average hours worked were some of the proposals put forward in the Unit's reports, but it was felt that none of these changes was likely to be really effective unless company management at all levels could be committed to working for agreed company objectives, and that these objectives could be broadly understood by non-management employees.

With the aid of consultants from the Tavistock Institute a statement of broad company objectives was formulated which were to be embodied in a participative and consultative style of management. The company accepted that, although its first aim must be to operate efficiently and profitably, it could not hope to buy greater job flexibility or any other desirable changes calculated to improve productivity except in a new framework of industrial relations. The new framework had to be one within which greater understanding and co-operation could be established between top management and other employees at all levels throughout the company. In drawing up a statement of company objectives the company also accepted that only if everyone understood the objectives and were committed to them was there any likelihood of their becoming effective, and that therefore this was not a matter simply of communication but of consultation and agreement. The statement when issued was put forward as a draft to be discussed not as a final communication of policy from the company to its employees. It was intended that the declaration when understood and accepted[1] would be a kind of constitution for the company—not a set of rules but a source of reference by which all major policy decisions and employment practices could be judged with the implication that action thought to run counter to the company's objectives would be 'unconstitutional' and could be queried and discussed. The company's objectives were worked out by a series of meetings with management, operatives and union representatives to discuss draft statements. One- and two-day conferences were held at intervals throughout 1965-7 to discuss the statement. One of the first practical steps in participative manage-

[1] i.e. accepted in general terms as a consistent style of management. Union representatives were never asked formally to enter into any agreements based on company policy documents.

ment was this encouragement given to junior staff to discuss frankly and critically and publicly a document put forward by top management. A number of study teams were initiated at the same time to discuss the implementation of specific proposals, e.g. single status for all employees.

Joint Working Parties were set up for craftsmen and for operators at each plant, through which it was intended that any new working arrangements could be thoroughly explored before any formal bargaining took place between management and unions, and which would exemplify the company's new approach to consultation with employees. A small addition (2d) to hourly rates was made to encourage the stewards to enter into discussions through the Joint Working Parties. This was later felt to be a mistake since it had to be withdrawn when the meetings of the working parties at one plant broke down. The management found that a pay reduction at a time of conflict in industrial relations could only exacerbate problems.

COMPANY OBJECTIVES

The first part of the company's statement of objectives contained many familiar items; there were the usual statements about the need to operate efficiently and to contribute to the overall profitability of the Group; to make good use of the community's resources (including preserving amenities), and to offer such opportunities for training and development for employees as would maximize their remuneration and job satisfaction and their contribution to the company's total efforts. Where the company believed that they were going further than is usual in declarations of company objectives was in stating unequivocally that the company is a steward of the community's resources to which it has privileged access and which it must manage and develop to meet society's needs for products and services.

The second part of the statement explained how the company proposed to begin to translate these laudable ideals into practice. Their plans were to be based upon the adoption of a concept, devised and presented to the company by its consultants, which they called 'joint optimization of the socio-technical system', that is an attempt to develop technological and human needs together so that in plant design, staffing and work organization the optimum balance could be achieved between technical excellence and employees' satisfaction. This involved a greater departure from current practices than at first may have appeared. In general a plant is designed and production is planned and only afterwards are people brought in to operate it. Similarly, general codes of good industrial relations may be sought without basing these effectively on the actual pattern of work which men and supervisors are called upon to undertake. The work of this company, for example, requires a labour force that is skilled, capable of continuous learning, and able in some situations to make decisions and accept responsibility for them. Its members must be able to appreciate something of the interrelation of their work with that of others in the company and in the Group although they will be remote from any direct connection with them. The company decided therefore that in planning its operations working practices must include some challenge and variety, some area of responsibility which each man can exercise in relation to his own work, some opportunities for updating skills, and some expectations for the future in terms of income, promotion and security. It was recognized that these needs would vary greatly between individuals and tasks, but it was felt that unless some of these needs were substantially met, men would tend to be frustrated and bored and unlikely to respond either to exhortation or money incentives alone in a way which would motivate them to commit themselves unreservedly to the company's objectives.

The drawing up of agreed objectives by discussion at all levels in the company, followed by continuous consultation about their implementation into working practices, was meant to be a demonstration of the company's sincere desire for a more participative style of management, and as a first exercise in getting company personnel involved in decision-making about the company's policies. The company recognized from the beginning that establishing participative management would be a lengthy process and that the changes initiated would not result in any instant harmony in industrial relations, nor necessarily in any immediately measurable results in increased productivity. During the three years (1965-8) some progress and some set-backs have occurred as a closer look at two of the company's plants shows.

In Plant A, whose history of poor industrial relations greatly influenced the company's decision to embark upon its new style of management, some progress had been made by 1967 in disseminating ideas about the company's objectives through a series of two-day conferences, and in preparing the way for a productivity deal. The representatives of the plant operators, who are T & G W U members, had co-operated with management through a Joint Working Party in discussing such changes as the introduction of single status and the end of 'clocking on'. They had also agreed to experimental re-manning of parts of the plant by 'block' teams which permitted a greater flexibility of working arrangements and which it was hoped could lead to a reduction of manpower and the elimination of habitual overtime. The main features of a productivity deal had been outlined by the end of 1967. These were a reduction in manpower and the elimination of extensive overtime, accompanied by guarantees about the spread and amount of 'call-in' time which management could demand, greater job flexibility, and a pay structure which would enable these savings to be effected without any serious drop in earnings. One difficulty in these discussions was that though the use of joint working parties was not meant in any way to by-pass the unions (it was always accepted that any final formal productivity bargain would be concluded through the usual management-union meetings) T&GWU wage agreements were usually negotiated at national level[1] and productivity bargains involve the kind of detail which can only be worked out plant by plant in a way which a national agreement cannot cover. T&GWU officers at national level were not willing to allow shop stewards too much power in negotiations with the company, and neither the stewards nor the company wanted to upset the agreed bargaining procedures and antagonize national union officials. The issue was then complicated by a national T&GWU claim for a 3 per cent across-the-board increase as a 'platform' for productivity bargains. This was rejected by the company as being an increase unrelated to any improvements in productivity and not consistent with national policies of wage restraint to which the company was subject. Further discussion of a productivity deal was frozen at this point and meetings of the Joint Working Party of operators were suspended. The threat which company and plant bargains appear to pose for traditional union power structures can create awkward obstacles to the development of productivity agreements.

The difficulty of keeping national and local negotiations in step did not arise in the case of craftsmen, but nevertheless greater difficulties were experienced in gaining their co-operation in joint consultation. The Joint Working Party of management and representatives of the craftsmen's Joint Union Negotiating Committee broke down and ceased to meet. The JUNC was led and dominated by one man who was sceptical of the company's sincerity, dismissed the new ideas of participative management as 'clap-trap' and made demands which the company found itself totally unable to consider. For example, a demand for guaranteed earnings of about £30 per week for all craftsmen would have meant an increase of £8 per week for some men for no additional work of productivity. These demands may have been put forward in order to provoke just such a response from management and provide a reason for withdrawal from the working

[1] This procedure was changed to company-level bargaining in 1967.

party. The objections of the craftsmen were not difficult to understand. They had developed a system of regular year-round overtime working on which they depended for their fairly high earnings and no shop steward or union official could contemplate agreeing to the reduction of this overtime unless completely reliable and predictable alternative working arrangements were made in which the company guaranteed in advance and without qualification that all craftsmen's earnings would be maintained. The JUNC were also not very cooperative about proposals to get rid of restrictive practices and demarcation rules, which they saw as a means of protecting the livelihood of their members and which could only be sold dear to the company with very secure safeguards. The craftsmen felt they stood to gain less from job flexibility (though in this they were probably mistaken) and, because they possessed skills which if necessary could be transferred elsewhere, they felt able to take a stronger stand against the management's proposals for change. They were less impressed by offers of joint consultation than their colleagues in the T & G W U, and some believed that participative management was simply a divide-and-rule policy which would enable management to manipulate employees at the expense of union influence and solidarity. The JUNC leaders, and they were not alone in this, were unhappy about the length of time involved in consultation and productivity discussions without any agreement emerging. They pointed out that if an agreement took a year to be reached the men had 'lost' the extra pay for a year and inflation would be likely to have reduced its original value anyway. In these circumstances men would lose confidence in the complexities of productivity bargaining and begin to press their representatives to put in a straight wage claim for an increase in hourly rates.

The initial lack of progress with the JUNC was a matter of considerable regret to the company because a bargain with craftsmen which included agreed procedures for calling men in as needed, rather than relying on prearranged voluntary overtime, could have enabled the company to improve the efficiency of the maintenance operations very substantially.

Although the craftsmens' and operators' unions bargained at different levels, neither of their senior shop stewards had any power to negotiate a deal with the company. Both men, being loyal unionists, accepted that only union officials could enter into formal negotiations; however, they complained bitterly that they would have to do all the real work involved in working out the time and job flexibility changes which would have to be embodied in an agreement, since local or national union officials could not possible be *au fait* with the particular situation at each plant. Paradoxically, these two senior shop stewards, who will have a decisive influence on the success or otherwise of the company's development programmes are at one time treated as equal partners in consultation with top management, and at other times as very junior employees with no status, whom some members of management may be not averse to cutting down to size when the opportunity offers. Some part of the suspicious awkwardness with which stewards approach meetings with management arises from their anomalous position in the organization and the conflict of roles they are called upon to play.

In addition to consultative machinery for craftsmen and operators, a joint working party was created with foremen and supervisors, and management set great store by getting supervisors to understand and implement the new management style since they were perhaps more immediately and directly affected by it than almost any other people in the company. Supervisors also appeared to have least to gain from the proposed changes. The introduction of single status and similar changes would eliminate the 'staff-works' distinctions which had in the past been part of their standing in the company, and changed working practices, like the end of 'clocking on', seemed likely to increase the need for supervisory checks on time-keeping. Some supervisors said rather sourly that they were at a disadvantage in the scramble to sell restrictive practices to management as they had never held back their services to the company, and they did not see how productivity could be measurable any way in their work. They acceded to the management's request to join in consultation and to try to implement the new style of supervision but some of them felt confused by the terminology used in discussing the new company philosophy (see p. 43 above) and some openly stated that they thought the meetings a distraction and a waste of time. Anxieties were aroused by some of the claims put forward at shop-floor level for workers to be represented on panels to appoint their supervisors. The initial effect of the new participative approach seemed to be to unsettle some supervisors who thought it would reduce their status and authority *viv-à-vis* the men they supervised, and would impose upon them a more demanding and less routine form of supervision. The proposed changes were said to be likely to give a considerable impetus to white collar unionism among supervisory staff.

The readiness of management to consult fully and frankly with employees about major company decisions was tested at the beginning of 1968 when it became necessary to announce the closing down of certain parts of the plant and a consequential run down of manpower. This followed a similar contraction in 1964 when a total of

420 employees were phased out over a period of six months. On this occasion, all employees over normal retirement age were retired and voluntary severance payments based on age and service were offered to those willing to terminate their service voluntarily with the company. Any operators could opt for voluntary termination, but among craftsmen the numbers had to be restricted within trade groups. This reduction of manpower was carried smoothly and there was no shortage of volunteers to take severance pay (or early pension and severance pay). Despite some uncertainties about eligibility for unemployment benefits and some confusing amendments to the original estimates of surplus jobs, the target figures were reached for operators and fell short by only a very small number for craftsmen. Employees appeared satisfied with the company's handling of the run down and the compensatory payments, but there was some residual mistrust among union representatives who described this scheme of severance payments as a 'diabolically clever' move on the part of management, and who resented the secrecy with which the accelerated wastage programme had been planned.

This experience in 1964 of redundancy, albeit sympathetically handled, and the fear of further reductions, no doubt influenced the attitudes of the men, especially the craftsmen, to the company's later proposals for a reorganization of certain working practices with the overall intention of reducing manning. Their anxieties thus appeared to be justified when it was announced at the beginning of 1968 that 313 jobs would have to be phased out as certain sections of the plant were to be shut down as uneconomic and no capital investment was immediately contemplated which would absorb this displaced manpower.[1]

The need to reduce manpower and the proposals to effect this between 1968 and 1970 were announced in a letter to all employees from the general manager, followed immediately by a meeting with representatives of all employee groups affected. It was contemplated that a number of further meetings could take place, as necessary, to discuss fully the implication of the run-down.

The letter gave the company's reasons for the decisions taken, and detailed the cost to company of retaining unnecessary labour (£400,000 to the end of 1970), contrasting it with the cost if the company simply declared a redundancy and only made payments due under the Redundancy Payments Act (£10,000). It set out the company's policy for dealing with the contraction of the labour force, viz. to make full use of natural wastage (retirement, resignations,

---

[1] In fact a year later the company took over an adjoining firm with a view to integrating operations and further reducing total manpower.

etc.) and to avoid recruitment which would increase the ultimate surplus of labour; to make transfers to other company locations where possible and accptable, and to offer generous voluntary severance payments (or early pension and severance payments). The precise calculation of rates of severance pay were to be made known later but, in any case, employees would have at least six months in which to consider their position before they had to make any decision; meanwhile details were given in the letter of the departments and jobs affected by the proposed shut-downs and the company promised to review the situation and its targets for de-manning at six-monthly intervals. The company finally gave a firm undertaking that there would be no redundancy declared until at least the end of 1970.

The announcement was not a complete surprise because the shut-down of certain departments had been expected for some time, but it had been hoped that new capital developments would have offset the contraction of other parts of the plant. The company have now made it clear that nothing of this kind is likely to happen before the end of 1971. The first announcement and certainly the first meeting to discuss it appeared to create very little interest and there was a very small attendance. The company's promise of no redundancy, the history of very fair severance payments given in 1964 and the generally satisfactory level of employment in the area, probably softened the blow considerably. A year later the run-down of surplus labour was proceeding satisfactorily in that there had been no serious objections raised by the men and their representatives, and no sudden increase in wastage rates which could have disorganized the company's production. The management have kept their undertaking to give frank six-monthly reviews of what jobs will be eliminated next, and by the beginning of 1969 the company was able to set out (by quarterly figures) the likely reductions up to the end of 1971 by which they hope to avoid having to declare an actual redundancy. (No one mentions the word redundancy if they can avoid it at this plant; the process is referred to euphemistically as 'accelerated wastage'.)

Alongside the labour run-down, discussions were continued to try and reach agreements for productivity deals with operators and craftsmen, and in April 1969, after a secret ballot, a productivity agreement with T & G W U members was agreed.

The craftsmen put in a claim for a straight wage increase which the company refused on the grounds that productivity proposals would be shortly submitted. Since the Joint Working Party had earlier broken down and the special payment for agreeing to participate in discussions had been forfeited, the company prepared a productivity

49

proposal unilaterally. After some months of argument a compromise about the forfeited payments was reached and negotiations are now proceeding on the productivity agreement.

The company has tried to keep to the terms of the new company philosophy by taking employees fully into management's confidence about this contraction of the labour force, but in the first place management made its decision unilaterally and without prior consultation, and it was based on the total business strategy of the Group. This might be objected to as contrary to the spirit of participative management and illustrates the difficulties which may arise unless the areas of company policy which are to be subject to consultation, and those which are not are quite clearly defined. If there are company decisions which are going to be reserved to top management, and/or to the board of the parent company, this needs to be made quite clear. If it is not, *any* decisions by the company not first discussed with employees may provoke confusion and distrust among employees who have been told that they are going to be consulted. Management by agreed objectives does not mean to this company an abdication of managerial initiative and responsibility for decision-making, though it should mean checking these decisions against the agreed objectives and being prepared to discuss and adopt their implementation in consultation with all those who are affected by them.

The second plant in which the idea of a new style of participative management was introduced had the advantage of planned expansion ahead, and changes did not have to be discussed against a background of possible redundancy. Management, in seeking to redeploy labour for more efficient use, was able to guarantee overall security of employment. On the other hand, it was a larger and more complex organization operating in an area with a traditionally militant labour force.

As at Plant A, staff at Plant B were released to attend conferences to discuss the new management concepts and their implications, and five joint working parties, including those with T&GWU members and with the craftsmen's JUNC, were set up. These were seen by management as fulfilling a separate long-term and on-going process of improving industrial relations and not simply as a prelude to specific productivity bargains, though the conclusion of these was expected to be tangible evidence of new ways in which management and employees could co-operate. At this plant top management felt that there had been too much peace-at-any-price and 'finger in the dyke' approaches to labour problems in the past, and they welcomed the idea of a longer-term approach based upon agreed company objectives. The company hoped to get co-operation in reducing over-manning and excessive overtime and in reducing demarcation rules which would make it possible to optimize the flexibility of jobs between craftsmen and between craft and non-craft operatives, and they were prepared to offer annual salaries, full staff status and guaranteed employment in return for the right to call in men for unpaid overtime as required within carefully defined limits.

The T&GWU shop stewards were ready to co-operate and began a dialogue with management, but they insisted on so much consultation with other sub-groups in order to keep everyone informed that excessive consultation exhausted members to no purpose, and eventually this approach petered out. Unfortunately, the Joint Working Party with the craft unions also broke down. The reactions of the craft unions were more militant and ended in a strike. When the company decided to eliminate charge-hands and promote some men to foremen supervisory grades, the question of their representation arose (since such changes could have important consequences for union membership). The JUNC for craftsmen insisted they continue to represent these men as their members together with all craft supervisors, although the supervisors in question were content to be represented by the staff association which they had then joined. Management would not yield to the JUNC's insistence on the presence of two of their shop stewards at discussions between the unions and management on representation claims. The JUNC instructed men to refuse to take instructions from supervisors unless they carried a craft union card and when some men carried out these instructions and were dismissed, the rest were called out on strike. The plant was operated by staff for four weeks before the men returned and joint working party meetings were not afterwards resumed.

The strike illustrated some of the problems which were likely to arise in any attempts to change working practices, even within a different management style, if these affect union membership and representation. The fact that promotion to supervisory grades gave staff status to former hourly-paid employees was not automatically regarded as a benefit by the men and their representatives. In this case, from the union's point of view the change was expected to lead to a loss of their membership (and dues) and a loss of power in the plant. Similarly, punching a time-clock is a management check on punctuality and attendance, but it is also the basis of claims for premium payments. Changes which are often advocated, like single status for all employees, including the end of 'clocking on', need careful consideration and preparation or they may be the cause of new disagreements.

The more management appeared to be dealing directly with groups of workers, and tackling grievances at an early stage, the more it seemed to union representatives that they might be by-passed in this process and their influence greatly reduced in this new style of company organization. The loss of some of their members, and the company's refusal to allow shop stewards to sit in on meetings with supervisors, appeared to confirm the unions' suspicions and made them sceptical of the company's readiness for full consultation. Some craftsmen were reluctant to contemplate the company's plans to reduce overtime, working and premium payments, but many were prepared to consider the proposals for a productivity agreement. At this point an overtime ban was applied by the craftsmen themselves (partly in order to bring pressure to bear on the company to improve their offer) and there was a temporary breakdown in negotiations.

From the beginning the craft unions were not much disposed to accept the ideas put forward at management conferences about the company's new development programmes, and to some extent the strike was a disengagement from closer relations with management. One of the chief JUNC representatives at this stage expressed the view that a closer embrace with management would lead to a kiss of death for the shop stewards. Unfamiliarity with the complexities of productivity bargaining and a fear of selling themselves short undoubtedly led to some unreasonable suspicions. The strike appeared to be a serious setback for the new management approach and critics were quick to point out that there had not been a strike for over ten years until the new company philosophy was introduced, and that this had produced very quickly a breakdown in labour relations.

One of the beneficial fall-outs of this unfortunate strike was that the position and responsibilities of management under the new dispensation were to some extent clarified. Consultative management had been shown to be not simply a question of giving way to any union demands and being nice to the men. Junior managers, particularly, learn to look at apparently beneficial changes more realistically from the point of view of the men and their representatives, and to realize that union support was not to be easily bought by taking shop stewards into the management's confidence—or their cloakrooms. Union representatives who had clamoured for consultation found that reasonable limits had to be set to the time and effort expended in trying to consult everyone with a possible interest in every decision.

The facts about uneconomic over-manning and overtime working and strict demarcation of jobs in the plant spoke for themselves when it was found that in practice the plant could be run by a much smaller labour force of *staff* during the strike. It was no doubt in part the improvement brought about by the new managerial attitudes which enabled discussions to be resumed again both with T&GWU stewards and the JUNC representatives without too much bitterness after the strike. The company avoided any temptations to view the end of the strike as a victory for management and continued to try to work out acceptable productivity deals. A package deal was put forward by the company which was aimed at taking care of the technological needs of the industry (twenty-four-hour plant operation), the business needs of the company (elimination of over-manning and excessive overtime) and the needs of the employees (status, security of earnings and limits set to the disturbance created by variable overtime requirements). Numerous problems arose out of this package deal on which it was to be expected that workers' representatives would want very careful assurances, for example the management's rights to call men in, the total amount of overtime to be worked and the period over which it was to be spread. Reluctance to agree that personal rates (which individual workers had been given for various reasons in the past) were to be brought into the new rates of annual salary also involved lengthy debate. The company were confident that there would be great savings by eliminating any incentives for men or supervisors to stretch overtime unnecessarily.

Savings were also expected in 'down' time because of the acceleration of minor maintenance jobs when teams of craftsmen and operators were working together. Operators under this system could be expected to have more incentive for plant care, and craftsmen could work as relief operators when no maintenance was required. The men and their representatives were brought fully into the detailed planning of availability rotas etc., and encouraged to take responsibility in the reorganization of tasks. Several months were allowed for preparation and transition to the new scheme during which it would be possible to deal with all the individual, often unforeseen, snags, which can develop and wreck agreements unless dealt with in advance.

Direct contacts through line management were relied upon to press the company's policy of consultation and maximum delegation of responsibility. A committee of shop stewards and a co-ordinating committee of management and stewards were set up to consider any problems arising which were not reserved for union negotiation. Under the new agreement, operatives and craftsmen were to have almost full staff status. Most were no longer clocking on (the experiment to end this practice having been successful), and all had equal sick pay and pension provision. The differences remaining were one week's less holiday and separate canteen accommodation.

Some supervisors were doubtful about the changes since they

appeared to reduce their responsibilities and authority, and some felt little benefit had emerged from interminable time-wasting discussions. The company recognized the problems created for their supervisors by the changes introduced, and hoped that the fact that they had backed up their supervisors even to the point of a strike (when they were pressed with unwanted union representation), together with a productivity deal yielding a 5 per cent increase in pay, would encourage supervisors to accept their new role as planners and organizers of the flow of work and its completion rather than as overseers of the labour force.

These and other problems had to be debated at considerable length. The shop stewards liked some parts of the package deal but not others but, since they were afraid of selling themselves short and agreeing to a deal which in the event gave management too much power, they were reluctant to come to a conclusion. The management were adamant that the deal could not be broken into pieces, some of it to be accepted and some rejected, and they were prepared to settle down to lengthy consultation to explain the company's minimum needs for an efficient operation of the plant which would at the same time yield higher and more secure earnings for their staff. The T & G W U stewards were allowed to concentrate full time on working through the problems and they were made more aware of the company's difficulties as they themselves tried to grapple with the complexities involved in the proposed changes.

The J U N C discussions became deadlocked because of a demand at first for all thirty-five and later for twenty-one shop-stewards to take part in the discussions, while management thought this was far too many, but discussions were eventually re-started and a productivity deal was signed with the craftsmen in August 1968 before agreement had been reached with the operators. The agreement embodied an annual salary, shift and special call-in allowances, time in lieu of overtime worked, work sharing between craftsmen and between craftsmen and operators, and training whenever it proved necessary to facilitate this. Fringe benefits were also automatically improved by being now related not to wage rates but to an annual salary. Few problems have arisen so far, and the Productivity Agreement Implementation Committee has been able to discuss those which have. An agreement for laboratory technicians has also been concluded successfully with U S D A W. The proposed agreement with the T & G W U followed similar lines and paid particular attention to training and career development for operators in the company. This has now been accepted after a secret ballot by the 2,000 T & G W U members.

In both Plants A and B the company had to try to introduce a new style of management against a background of rather unsatisfactory industrial relations and considerable suspicions built up over the years among shop stewards, especially craftsmen, who, not surprisingly, wanted guarantees that the earnings and the interests of their members would not be adversely affected by any changes. When, however, in 1968 the company opened a new plant it was possible to attempt from the beginning to implement the new style of management. A smaller labour force of carefully selected operators were given six months training, and maintenance by craftsmen was subcontracted out which for the time being by-passed any difficulties which might have been raised by craftsmen about the pattern of greater job flexibility.

Under an agreement with the T&GWU (December 1966) all employees at the new plant have the same terms for holidays, sick pay, etc., and the General Manager queues with the rest of his staff for meals in a joint canteen. All operatives work a 40-hour week spread over three shifts with unpaid overtime restricted to an absolute minimum, and with time in lieu of such periods that have to be worked. It is intended that the need to give such time in lieu will discipline supervisors and managers in the use of overtime and the planning of their work.

The annual salary plus shift allowances compares very favourably with earnings by operatives in other plants in the industry. To honour the company's promises about training men to learn as many jobs as possible in the five operator grades and then to be able to slot these men into suitable vacancies means that, when account is taken of holiday arrangements and sickness absence, the company needs a 10 per cent additional staff load to keep three shifts working, and on these terms its labour has to be very highly productive to offset its costs.

There was little enthusiasm at the beginning among the trainees for union membership, but they were encouraged by the company to belong to their union and the company arranged to check off their union dues from their salary at source, and encouraged the men to elect shop stewards. At this point, while the men were waiting to try out their deal with the management when the plant became fully operative, no need seemed to be felt on either side for any further machinery for consultation or representation, but this might change if problems arise later.

After three and a half years, what has been achieved by this attempt to manage by agreed company objectives, and at what cost? From the company's point of view the direct cost of conferences and consultants had been about £60,000, together with the indirect cost of company time spent by managers, especially at senior levels. It is not possible to cost this precisely, but at both locations the time and effort spent on implementing the company's new philosophy has not had any adverse effect on their operations and output. The process of conference and discussion and productivity bargaining has involved many more people in taking responsibility than would have been the case in a more authoritarian system of management and proved to be in itself a form of management training which has added to the education and development of staff at all levels. Some of the cost of the procedures for introducing the company's new management style might otherwise have been spent on sending managers outside the company for training. New and better channels of communication have been developed throughout each plant between and within departments and across organizational frontiers because staff in all departments have been encouraged to discuss and challenge company policy, and in so doing to look outside their own section or department at the activities of the company as a whole.

The successful implementation of changes in working practices, e.g. the agreements to end clocking-on and the pilot projects based on job flexibility and de-manning, prepared the way for major productivity deals which have been signed at one location and are near to completion at another. The productivity negotiations have been long drawn out, but no more so than similar agreements in other industries which have taken two to three years. On the other hand, the introduction of the new management style and the exercise in defining company objectives did not accelerate agreement noticeably or prevent the demand, arising from union suspicions, for guaranteed earnings. Joint consultation machinery has been overhauled to make it more meaningful to employees at shop-floor level, and management believe they are tapping reserves of intelligence and ability hitherto unused as more employees understand the company's objectives and programmes.

It is difficult to evaluate the effects of the company's new management style, until it has been operating for a longer time. It will be some time, for example, before the yield of the productivity deals can be calculated or any judgement made as to whether industrial relations are consistently better. It is, however, possible to see how the new style of participative management has enabled the company to deal with situations which have put the new company relationships under considerable strain. One location has had a strike, and the other is involved in contracting its labour force, and both locations have been deadlocked in their discussions with shop stewards, as they have tried to evolve a way of reducing overtime and over-manning without causing an unacceptable drop in earnings. Neither the strike nor the redundancy has prevented the company from keeping negotiations going which have produced some far-reaching changes in working practices[1] now embodied in three productivity agreements and a fourth under discussion. In doing this they have had to secure the agreement of shop stewards who were initially deeply suspicious and sceptical about the company's development plans, and notwithstanding that the new style of consultation was neither understood by nor acceptable to everyone on the management side of the company.

The leadership of the JUNC at Plant A remained during the first three years unconvinced of the benefit to be derived from the new forms of consultation. Initially they demanded a guarantee from the company of higher earnings in advance of any certainty that greater productivity could result and without this reassurance they were not willing to continue the meetings of the Joint Working Party. The management however persevered in their attempts to reach agreement and subsequent to a change of union leadership negotiations were begun again with craftsmen.

Some supervisors are uncertain of the value of the new management style which makes greater demands on their managerial skills and which they fear may reduce their former status and authority in the company. Some feel that the hourly-paid workers, who have not always been wholly co-operative with management, are now being wooed with offers of better status and remuneration, while supervisors who have loyally served the company's interests and never operated restrictive practices now have nothing to 'sell' to the company. Numbers of supervisors who had not considered this possibility before, now say they must protect their interests by joining 'white collar' unions. Will the company find that the improvement in relations with manual workers is partly offset by some discouragement of staff? When one group of workers in an enterprise negotiate any improvement in pay and conditions, others will argue also for improvements even if they are as well off as similar workers elsewhere, and they have not been asked to change their working practices; 'long standing relativities in an industry are important'.[2] The company has tried to meet these dissatisfactions by new agreements with technicians and supervisors.

[1] Some of these, e.g. in elimination of overtime, may prove to be resented by some young vigorous workers who see overtime as the only way to enhance their earnings at this period of their working lives. It is too soon to say whether this will cause them to seek unlimited working arrangements elsewhere.

[2] See also Professor Sir Ronald Edwards, *An Experiment in Industrial Relations: The Electrical Supply Industry's Status Agreement for Industrialized Staff*, published by the Electricity Council, 1967.

Some of the supervisors, as well as shop stewards, have complained that the new ideas of company purpose and consultation were expressed in a form they found difficult to understand, and they have complained of 'jargon' which did not seem very relevant to their immediate workshop problems. These objections tended to disappear as the policy was implemented in very detailed agreements and men began to see tangible results, but it was not easy to embody the new concepts in a practical and easily recognizable form for some clerical and supervisory staff.

The fact that the top management of the company and the senior staff at each plant location unequivocally accepted and persevered with the new style of management in the face of not a little opposition and misunderstanding they believe has made possible some progress in improving the general quality of industrial relations in the company. The gains have been slowly made and may take some time to consolidate but barriers of suspicion have been sufficiently lowered to make possible productivity deals, involving substantial changes in traditional working practices, which the management are satisfied will lead to a much more efficient use of resources.

The most significant effect of this type of essay in participative management is the clarification of the roles of management and unions and supervisors. Words like participation can only too easily become vague and meaningless if not a fruitful source of misunderstanding. The company has made quite clear their view that this does not represent any reduction of managerial responsibility and that this is not a form of co-determination or co-direction of the company. On the other hand the shop stewards and union representatives have a secure, central and recognized place in consultation and negotiation which they believe is likely to be far more effective than a representative on a remote board,[1] and the company have not set up any procedures which have by-passed the unions even though productivity deals have been held up for lengthy periods by what appeared to the management to be union intransigence. Both in the productivity deals and in all other fringe benefits and working conditions everything which can be reduced to agreed procedures (especially where any grievance or dispute is concerned) has been spelt out in advance in considerable detail so that managerial discretion, which to employees often looks like arbitrariness, is minimized. The changes made (ending 'clocking-on', payment by annual salaries, etc), which remove discrepancies between staff and works, and the fact that dismissals and disputes must be dealt with by agreed

---

[1] Bearing in mind the structure of the group of companies of which this is a part. See p. 40 above.

procedures, will enhance the status of manual workers. The company has made no promises about security of employment which it is unlikely to be able to keep, but it recognizes obligations for advance notice of redundance, generous severance pay and help in retraining and finding alternative employment. The productivity deals were not gestures in welfare; they were reciprocal agreements in which operators were asked to give up traditional working practices in return for a different pattern of pay and work offered by the company.

The aim of getting everyone committed to the company's objectives, with its association of company loyalty, is an aspect of this exercise that raised some doubts especially among unionists. Can the company's interests and the workers' interests be kept so harmoniously in step? The company believed that with more understanding and information about the company's aims, employees would see that they have a common interest in the company's prosperity. This may be true in the long run but there are almost certain to be conflicts of interest in the short run. No one has ever supposed that participative management based on defined company objectives would wholly eliminate conflicts, but it is hoped that conflicts can be contained with less bitterness within the procedures available to settle disputes.

As far as democratizing the organization is concerned the impact may prove to be strongest among middle and junior management, where the delegation of responsibility and the encouragement of the Young Turks has been very noticeable in producing a continuous critical review of the company's aims and performance.

The response to participation by operatives is not easy to ascertain and it may prove only a minority have a sustained response to this approach in the long run. Workshop involvement and responsibility may not be as universally desirable to workers as has sometimes been supposed. Studies of workers in certain industries[1] have emphasized the tendency observed there for many men to regard work in a largely instrumental manner as the means to the enrichment of a life outside work and centred upon the home and family. Such men may have no particular need for a sense of belonging to the organization for which they work, no deep feelings of solidarity with workmates, and suffer no intolerable deprivation if they get only partial job satisfaction. They may be satisfied to stay with a company if it yields the level of wages they want without having in any way closely identified with the organization.[2] The industries in which this may be currently true, e.g. in car assembly and the building industry,

[1] Goldthorpe et al., *The Affluent Worker*, Cambridge University Press, 1968.
[2] See also Chapter 4.

are not necessarily typical of all industry. However, if this trend did prove to be true increasingly of other industries in future, the attempts of a company to see its labour relations in terms of participation and commitment to the company's objectives might prove inappropriate for at least some of its work force whose main interests are extrinsic to the work place, though this does not mean that it will not be worth while for the rest.

The development of participative management may appear to have only a very limited and indirect effect on the pattern of company control. To the extent that it has led to genuinely less autocratic and hierarchical systems of industrial management, the independence and status of workers have been enhanced and the opportunities for bringing forward their needs increased. But there is no evidence to show whether or not it will lead to any enthusiasm by them to participate in company decision-making, and it is probably unreasonable, especially if there is increased labour mobility, to expect that it should. The emphasis seems likely to be upon direct workshop involvement rather than indirect involvement in general company policy and for the rest most workers will continue to rely upon their union representatives to protect their interests, and will feel that the best way to ensure that companies are forced to take account of their interests is by having skilled and professional union services to represent them.

Where some real change in the sharing of managerial responsibility for company decision-making can already be discerned, and is likely to be further encouraged by more consultative styles of company organization, is among the ranks of middle and junior management. These include people who have already shown a capacity for exercising responsibility, and who say they welcome the opportunity to make a greater contribution. If more of the decisions of top management were open to prior discussion and challenge within the company this could significantly influence company board control in addition to affecting the efficiency of the company and the incentives and job satisfaction of managers.

Chapter 3

Case Study II: Security of Employment in the Construction Industry

The construction industry is a fertile field for enquiry into companies' social responsibilities since it is generally considered to be an industry where there is little consideration for employees' rights. Most importantly, the labour force is thought to be chronically casual and employers are often castigated as socially irresponsible because the traditional hire and fire policies allow them to draw arbitrarily on a pool of labour for which they accept no long-term commitment to provide continuity of employment. Moreover, fringe benefits which are taken for granted in other industries, such as pensions and sick pay, are either not provided at all or provided only to a very limited extent. Similarly, amenities are provided only to a very low basic standard. Of course the Contracts of Employment Act, the Redundancy Payments Act and the relevant Factory Acts operate in this industry as in every other, but a superstructure of fringe benefits built on statutory requirements is generally lacking in the construction industry.

It was therefore unusual to find in this industry a large company, with over 10,000 operatives, whose board made it clear, by practice and public statement, that they felt it to be an employer's social responsibility to alleviate the effects of some of these evident disadvantages on their operatives. In the context of their industry this particular company felt it to be their responsibility and also to their long-term economic advantage to offer three major groups of benefits to their operatives which are not provided by most of their competitors.

The first unusual benefit offered is that of more stable employment for those who want it. The company's handbook, given to each man as he signs on, states:

'Throughout the Group there are opportunities for satisfactory workers to obtain continuous employment. Long service records are numerous and there is every encouragement and scope for workers, whatever their positions, to earn promotion to higher grades and greater responsibility. Many of the managers, foremen and others started from the bottom and have lifelong service in this organization.'

To make good this policy the company offers operatives a transfer to another site where possible when the contract on which they are working can no longer employ them. It also operates a 'key man' scheme whereby men whose work is satisfactory are offered continuous employment as of right and a merit plus-rating of 3d to 6d per hour. For all operatives in or out of the key-man scheme, length of service brings a limited immunity from dismissal. After three years' continuous service the consent of a visiting manager (a senior staff man responsible for the supervision of several sites) is required before an operative may be dismissed. In practice, it was found that this was a very potent defence for an operative, since site managers found it much easier to transfer an unsatisfactory operative than argue the case for dismissing him with a visiting manager.

Secondly, the company has a contributory pension scheme for its operatives, and workers with five years' service, or a key man with two years' service, may join. In addition, the company provides benefits ranging upwards from £200 on the death of an employee not a member of the pension fund but with over one year's service. Key men are paid during sickness absence and the company, which has for many years sought to relieve hardship during illness by making voluntary payments, has formally promised to continue doing so. (The company's records show that this undertaking has been honoured.)

Thirdly, the company makes extra efforts to which it is not compelled by statute, to maintain safe sites, good canteens and other amenities. This is particularly true in the case of industrial safety in that operatives are positively encouraged to complain if any part of the company's promise to provide safe working conditions is being neglected.

The provision of a degree of continuous employment is obviously the most important and the most unusual, at least in the primary construction sector of the building industry, where discontinuity of work makes this provision extremely difficult. Our enquiry was therefore concentrated on estimating the effectiveness of this policy. Security of employment was studied in the general context of the company's aims, to try to establish both how far the company's scheme could be said to meet the worker's interests, and how far it satisfied the usual criteria for judging labour costs, i.e. by the effects upon the price and quality of services that can be offered to the consumer, and the return to the suppliers of risk capital. Also, building companies' use of manpower has to be considered from the point of view of its impact on the economy as a whole, particularly as the construction industry is labour intensive.

BENEFITS TO THE EMPLOYEES ACCRUING FROM THE COMPANY'S CONCEPT OF SOCIAL RESPONSIBILITY

The first part of the enquiry was directed towards finding out how employees themselves view the company's labour policies.

Following a small pilot enquiry, between June and November 1967, 371 men were interviewed on five construction sites to explore their attitudes towards working in a 'casual' industry, and their reactions to the company's efforts to decasualize employment and improve working conditions. On four of these sites, 1,057 records relating to current employees, and 3,005 relating to former employees paid off, were examined for any light they could throw on the pattern of labour turnover.

The operatives interviewed were a random 1 in 5 sample on two of the company's larger sites and the total labour force on three smaller sites. Two sites were in the metropolitan area and one near to London (twenty miles), and two were in the North. Three contracts were for municipal housing (some of it industrialized building), one was an office block and one a civil engineering motorway development. They represented a fair cross-section of the primary construction contracts likely to be undertaken by a large multi-regional company in the industry.

The interviewees' answers to questions have to be set against the industrial environment in which they work and their wage structure. (Nearly all the men interviewed volunteered to explain the nature of the industry and the payments system on the grounds that their answers might otherwise not be understood by the interviewer.)

Conditions vary enormously and indeed the construction industry is heterogeneous to the point that the only thing certain sections of it have in common are the materials they use.

Firms in the construction industry are engaged in traditional and industrialized building, civil engineering projects of varying size and complexity and in repairs and maintenance. In addition, some constructional companies are property developers and landlords. The range of work undertaken varies from minor repair jobs on private dwellings to large motorway contracts. It is estimated (Ministry of Public Building and Works, 1966) that 40 per cent of the industry's labour force is engaged in repairs and maintenance, and the remaining 60 per cent on new work. Just over 70 per cent of the total output of the industry is in primary construction.

As might be expected from this diversity some parts of the labour force are less 'casual' than others and the extent and incidence of the high labour turnover thought to be characteristic of the industry as a whole is confined to some parts of it, mainly that part concerned with primary construction.

Of the 1.6 million labour force some 81,000[1] are 'self-employed owners, managers, partners, etc., who do manual work' as distinct from operative employees. Of the remaining 1,519,000 some 363,000 (24 per cent) are in the employ of local authorities. In this sector, where much of the work is maintenance, labour turnover is less than the average for most industries, amounting to 30 per cent a year, and stability is high, with 81 per cent of operatives having more than one year's service and nearly half with more than five years' service. Thus the men in the employ of local authorities are not really 'casually' employed. If the operatives employed by the local authorities are deducted this brings the total potential 'casual' force employed by private contractors down to about 1.1 million men.

While on the one hand there has been a trend in recent years for more men to be employed in larger firms (one-fifth are now in firms with more than 1,200 employees), there has also been a trend towards more self-employment and 'labour-only' sub-contracting. The latter is a working system in which a sub-contractor provides only labour as distinct from the usual 'supply and fix' sub-contractor who provides equipment and materials as well.

The Phelps Brown Committee found, as would be expected, a correlation between labour turnover, labour stability and size of contracts. (Labour turnover is defined as the total number of leavers during a year expressed as a percentage of the average number employed during the year; and labour stability as the number with more than one year's service as a percentage of the number employed.) They also found a relationship between labour turnover and size of company, which is probably only another facet of the same variable because on the whole only larger companies tend to have the capital resources and management expertise to undertake large contracts.

In firms with less than 1,200 employees (which covers at least 77 per cent of the labour force working for private contractors), 73 per cent of operatives were not contributing to the annual turnover

[1] *Report* of the Committee of Enquiry under Professor E. H. Phelps Brown into certain matters concerning Labour in Building and Civil Engineering, HMSO, Cmnd. 3714, 1968.

figures. The turnover was being produced by only 27 per cent of that labour force. Given that 73 per cent of the labour force had stayed at least one year with one employer (and 31 per cent over five years) employment in this sector of the industry can hardly be said to be casual.

On the other hand in the larger firms, with over 1,200 employees, stability rates may be lower and turnover rates higher than the Report suggests. There are about eighty-five firms with more than 1,200 employees but some nine of these firms probably employ half the labour force or approximately 110,000 operatives (10 per cent of all those working for private contracts). The firm in which the present study was carried out is one of the nine largest firms, and reports that it has an annual average labour turnover rate of 200 per cent, and that about 28 per cent of their operatives have been in their employ for more than two years. Figures from other large companies as well as the results of the survey of operatives in this firm suggest that, with or without benefit of a stabilization policy, 25–30 per cent of their operatives have been with them for one year or more, and that turnover rates are about 200 per cent.

It can therefore be seen from these figures that about 250,000 operatives (some 16 per cent of the industry's total labour force including local authority employees etc.) are in firms with over 1,200 employees. Of these probably half (some 8 per cent of the industry's labour force) are the employees of the very largest firms with operative labour forces ranging from 6,500 to over 20,000. Given the correlation between increasing size and decreasing stability, it is possible to infer the following:

(a) the stability rate (proportion of men who have more than one year's service) in firms employing over 1,200 people, but not in the top nine giants, is probably about 60 per cent so that some 75,000 employees did not change jobs last year; and

(b) the nine giant firms probably have a stability rate of about 30 per cent so that a further 37,500 employees did not change jobs last year.

If these two stable groups are added together, i.e. 112,500 men, and also the labour force used by local authorities and smaller firms where operatives are two-thirds or more stable is disregarded, the remaining 10 per cent of the industry's labour force (about 160,000 men) appear to be responsible for the great part of high turnover figures in the whole industry. Moreover, they are a stage army appearing and reappearing in the turnover figures of a number of companies. This 10 per cent also makes another entrance from time

65

to time as part of the labour-only sub-contracting gangs. The self-employed are a distinct group but the labour-only force is also intermittently (and sometimes concurrently)[1] part of the employed operative force. There are some labour-only sub-contractors who work consistently in this way exclusively, but a considerable number of them move in and out,[2] undertaking short spells of work with friends as attractive opportunities present themselves. They are confident of getting themselves re-engaged by regular construction firms since men readily accepted into labour-only gangs are generally recognized to achieve above-average productivity.

None of these calculations is intended to suggest that labour turnover is not important, but merely to show the nature and the incidence of the problem, and the extent to which the conclusions of this survey can be applied to the industry. Only 26 per cent of interviewees had been in the employ of the company studied for more than three years; and, of the remainder, 59 per cent had changed employers between once and three times over the last three years and the remaining 15 per cent had changed employers more than three times. The work histories of individual employees included employment with nearly every large company in the industry and employees appeared to make no distinction between different large 'national' companies as employers. The conclusions drawn from the interviews are, therefore, broadly applicable to 10 per cent of the operative labour force engaged in primary construction for large multi-regional contractors and probably also to operatives working for other slightly smaller but still sizeable firms (i.e. more than 1,200 employees). High turnover and low stability are concentrated in this area of the industry, and it is here, if anywhere, that the 'casual' nature of employment may give cause for serious concern.

It is also important to understand the nature of this turnover. In brief, it is largely voluntary, not directly caused by employers withdrawing jobs, but by operatives themselves deciding to leave. The Phelps Brown Report produced various estimates of how many men leave their jobs voluntarily and concluded that in firms with over 1,200 employees about two-thirds quit as compared with one-third who are dismissed. In this survey if men transferred to other sites with the same company are included, the percentages for total pay-offs on all sites were 80 per cent quits, 16 per cent dismissals and 4 per cent transfers, and the averages of the percentages in these categories on the four sites were 65 per cent quits, 25 per cent dismissals and 10 per cent transfers.

[1] See Phelps Brown *Report*, para. 372, p. 134.
[2] See work histories of men interviewed below.

Thus the length of contracts is not by itself responsible for the amount of mobility in this sector of the industry, neither indeed do dismissals account for the greater part of job changes. The survey figures (even if an unusually low figure for Site 2 is excluded) do not indicate at most more than 33 per cent rate of dismissals. In the main, men were leaving voluntarily, or quasi-voluntarily (since these figures undoubtedly conceal some men who would have been dismissed if they had not quit first). The timing of turnover is also significant. Most of it occurs at an early stage of employment. Analysis of the four sites showed that 19 per cent of all pay-offs left within the first week of employment and a further 56 per cent within the first three months. The 19 per cent leaving within the first week represented largely a sorting out procedure due to the way in which the industry recruits labour. If selection procedures were improved this 19 per cent of turnover could probably be reduced, but the adverse consequences for less skilled and experienced labour would have to be weighed against any benefits gained.

The great variation in the rates both of dismissals and quits between sites was a function of the local labour markets. One of the sites which had a very high percentage (87 per cent) of voluntary quits was awkwardly placed for transport facilities in relation to the local labour available, and many other large building projects, some more conveniently situated, were in progress in the area. As a result, recruitment was difficult and men recruited tended to quit after a few days, before site management had had time to establish whether these new starters were unsuitable or not, i.e. the dismissal rate would have been a good deal higher if men had stayed long enough to be dismissed. Moreover, this site was at several stages in the contract so desperate for labour that management were reluctant to dismiss any men who were even partially useful.

There are structural reasons for high labour turnover owing to circumstances and problems peculiar to the construction industry. These structural reasons fall into four groups: the unavoidable discontinuities of work encountered by employers, the technology of the industry, the nature of the industry's pay-structure, and the methods of recruitment employed in the industry.

Discontinuity of work
A substantial degree of labour turnover is probably unavoidable in construction as at present organized, owing to structural discontinuities in the work. Contracts must come to an end and, in the present system of competitive tendering, companies cannot be certain of continuous work in the same area. No company needs to be

67

exhorted to try and maintain continuity of work in one area. Quite apart from the needs of operatives there is every incentive to secure continuity in order to use plant effectively and to minimize disturbance for key staff, but companies have to operate where the work is, and many large civil-engineering projects like motorways or power stations are 'one off' and not likely to be repeated in a nearby area.

A recent enquiry[1] into arrangements which would allow contractors to plan greater continuity in road building has found that serial contracting cannot be recommended as it yields no financial benefit. Increased costs would outweigh any possible savings. Over the next two years there seems little prospect of arranging many 'long' contracts for trunk and motorway schemes without unacceptable delays. The maximum scope for future 'long' contracts is assessed as 15 per cent to 25 per cent of total motorway and trunk road programmes. The report does, however, suggest that some contracts could be larger and longer for one road section or for series of projects in one locality in the interests of greater continuity of employment.

It would help companies to some extent if, as the Phelps Brown Report suggests, authorities could estimate the future flow of public work in each area. However, the usefulness of such a proceeding is strictly limited. There is no constraint on government to carry out their published plans and the construction industry, with more than half its orders coming from government, suffers immediately and directly in any economic set-back and from cuts in public expenditure and credit restrictions which create fluctuations in demand beyond the control of the industry. Even if governments could estimate total spending accurately and keep to their estimates this would not help individual companies, while competitive tendering is maintained. Any recommendation that open tendering (where the lowest tender must be accepted) should go, and more closed tendering be used, will discriminate against companies not on the tender list, and lay those companies on the list open to the temptation to divide the market up between them. This might well enable companies to stabilize their labour forces but could have other serious economic disadvantages.

Already large companies adopt a policy of regionalization. The company investigated in this survey had four divisions which were further sub-divided into regions. This helped to some extent in stabilizing staff as it meant that they could be allocated to an area, albeit a large one, but its usefulness was limited for operatives. The

[1] 'Report of the Joint Consulting Team on Serial Contracts for Road Construction', prepared for the Ministry of Transport by Business Operations Research Limited and Associated Industrial Consultants Limited, August 1967 (unpublished).

regions were so large that operatives might still have to accept living away from home or very long daily journeys to work. Any further regionalization in the company investigated would lead to expensive duplication of administrative staff. It seems therefore that, short of radical changes in the present competitive tendering system, some discontinuity of work in this sector of the industry is structural and cannot easily be altered.

The rate of labour turnover, however, remains higher than can be explained by these discontinuities. The company investigated estimated that their average contract takes eighteen months to complete and probably could provide a year's work for everyone hired (fewer men are required to start and finish a contract than when it is running at its peak).

The technology of the construction industry

The effect of the technology of the industry on labour turnover is also critical. This is an industry where the techniques are fairly standard. This is not to say that all men can do the same job but a joiner specializing in shuttering will find the work he is expected to do will not vary much from site to site. Men can therefore move from job to job without causing major difficulties for their employer, or losing a percentage of their own earnings while they learn the next job. Essentially the job for a particular man is always much the same; it is only the location which is different.

The pay structure

An operative's pay packet is made up of four elements:

(1) Basic pay for forty hours' work, which amounts to about £13 for labourers (6s 5d per hour London rate) and £15 for craftsmen (7s 5½d an hour London rate).

(2) Premium pay for overtime hours, ranging from time and a quarter to double time on Sundays. On building sites in the company investigated it was unusual for a man to do more than ten hours' overtime since there are statutory regulations limiting the hours to fifty a week and a certificate is required to allow a site to work longer. On civil engineering projects, however, as many as twenty or thirty overtime hours are regularly worked, and overtime premium starts at time and a half.

(3) Bonus payments under incentive schemes. Effectively all companies with over 1,200 employees use an incentive scheme, although this is not true of many smaller companies and some specialist contractors. It is generally accepted that men should be

69

able to get up to one-third of their basic pay in incentive pay, which would give labourers around £4 and craftsmen £5 per week.

(4) Payments for travelling time and fares. In London men get their fares and a lump sum which is related to how far they travel and is laid down in their Working Rule Agreement. Outside London men get fares and a time allowance for travelling. Craftsmen also receive small sums (2s a week generally) as a depreciation allowance on their tools and small amounts such as boot allowances are also paid where appropriate. All these amounts are regulated by Working Rule Agreements.

Items 1 and 4 in the pay packet remain more or less constant, at any rate between nationally negotiated changes. Items 2 and 3, however, can and do vary widely between site and site (and even between different sections of the same site). Overtime varies greatly. The difference to a craftsman on a building site working two hours' overtime and working ten can be nearly £4 a week, and in civil engineering the differentials are much wider. Bonus payments of course vary even more. An incentive scheme works on 'targets'. Every operation is targeted, i.e. a time allowance is given for it. For example, in the company investigated, one-and-a-half hours were allowed for the hanging of an internal softwood door. If the job was finished in an hour, the man received a 'bonus' (typically) of 50 per cent of his rate for the time he had saved. Targets are set so that most men can earn bonus; they were based, in the company studied, on what is called 60 performance efficiency per hour which most men could easily achieve. It is accepted that bonus is not an extra but part of the regular pay packet (as evidenced by the provisions in the national agreement that men should get 33 per cent of their basic wage in bonus). Bonus payments vary from site to site for three main reasons, only one of which has anything to do with productivity.

First, bonus payments vary directly with the targets set. The company studied had built up a bank of work study data which gave standard targets for most operations, and other large companies have similar data but, since this information is not shared, targets may vary widely between different companies' sites for particular operations. In any case company policy varies. In two divisions of the company studied, local site management may not change a company performance target without consultation with regional management. At least two other giant firms in the industry leave this particular aspect of management largely in the hands of site management, with the overall proviso that their agents (an agent is a site manager) achieve their profit targets, and this leads to great variations in targets set and in the consequent earnings available to operatives.

Secondly, bonus payments vary with the state of the local labour market. Adjustment of bonus targets provides the quickest and most flexible response to the market situation. The evidence for this is patent in London, where average bonus is about twice that in the rest of the country, and there is no reason to believe that London labour is twice as productive; in fact many experienced managers suggest that, on average, London labour is less so.

Thirdly, bonus earnings vary with site organization. On a well-organized site, men can earn more bonus even if the targets are unaltered. Factors like the placing of materials, tidiness of site and working distances involved make a great difference to bonus earnings. These are not factors over which operatives have much control; if an operative finds himself on a poorly organized site he is likely to feel he cannot do much to reorganize his work single-handed and thereby improve his bonus earnings. The only way he sees to increase his productivity and earnings is to quit and find a better site.

Thus there are two variable elements in the pay packet: overtime earnings and bonus. The degree of variation and the proportion of the pay packet made up by bonus is substantial. Figures for one area (Site 3) demonstrate this:

Number of men	Average weekly gross pay	Average bonus	Average basic	Average overtime at 1¼
56	£22 3s 6d	£5 19s	£13 19s 6d	£2 5s

Note: Many men received non-taxable fares and tool allowances in addition to this amount.

The table shows that the variable section of the pay packet, bonus and overtime, amounts to £8 4s, or 37 per cent of total pay. Any variation in this large percentage obviously makes a great overall difference, and the effect from an operative's point of view is that he may be able to increase his earnings by about 25 per cent simply by changing sites.

Method of recruitment

The method of recruitment is essentially casual on most large sites. Men arrive at the site office and if they look reasonably healthy and have a National Insurance card they are 'given a start'. A man is accepted as a skilled or plus-rated operative on his word but will be fired within the week if he turns out to be unable to do the job. This

71

goes far to account for the 19 per cent of all turnover that happens in the first week of a man's employment. It also means that this figure includes some men really incapable of holding down any job, who get a couple of days work on a site to get some ready money or to prove, in order to claim unemployment benefits, that they are genuinely 'capable, available and ready for work'.

In this connection it should be noted that as labour is recruited and used at present, the industry can absorb and make use of men with few, if any, definable skills. If recruitment to the industry were to be formalized, and not only craftsmen but all employees occupationally graded, given trade tests, and asked to fill up forms when applying for jobs, some men currently working acceptably in the industry would be excluded. At present the extreme informality of recruitment gives a man a chance to show what he can do, and while this means firms hire some men they have to fire in a day or two, it also means that capable men without formal training have a chance to show what skills they have and that they can learn quickly on the job.

THE INTERVIEWS

To explore the influence of these and other factors on voluntary leaving and to study the response of operatives to the company's offer of stable employment, 371 men were interviewed on five company sites.

This company at present offers two different employment patterns to its operatives: short-term stability, i.e. employment for the duration of the contract; and long-term stability i.e. permanent service in the company. But these are not mutually exclusive as one main objective of long-term security is to influence short-term stability. In offering short-term stability the company offers all competent workers (a) a good[1] bonus in addition to the basic rates, (b) good[1] welfare amenities, and (c) the promise of work on a following contract where possible. In offering long-term stability the company offers, in addition, prospects of promotion, pension and other service-related benefits, and generally slightly higher[1] wage rates. This operates through the key men and other schemes and probably by a more generous interpretation of allowances and rates for special circumstances.

The conditions on which the company offers short-term stability are the same conditions (as to competence, discipline and working conditions) as apply to a man to whom the company offers long-term stability, with the important addition that the latter must be prepared

[1] That is rather better than the average in the industry.

to travel at the company's convenience. This is not an absolute rule; operatives who are not prepared to live away from home may be useful to the company for some years if the company has a long run of work in one area. However, bearing in mind the purposes for which the company requires long-term stability, a long-service operative who is not prepared to travel is not serving the purpose for which he has been kept on the company's pay-roll; and most long-service men will at some stage have to accept periods of living away from home. The interviews were therefore primarily directed towards motivation; why do men in this industry change jobs so frequently and what are their feelings about security of employment?

On the largest sites (Sites 2 and 5) a sample of 1 in 5 (ninety-four and ninety-five men respectively) were interviewed. The sample was random except for seventeen of the ninety-three Sikhs on Site 5 who were selected for their capacity to be interviewed in English. Every man on the smaller sites was interviewed. Attendance at interviews was carefully stated to be voluntary and the interviewer felt she talked to only two men who were unwilling to discuss any questions with her.

Men were interviewed individually and in private on site; interviews were structured round a check list of questions and a schedule for each man was completed immediately after each interview. Many answers were unprompted as men, in discussing their work histories, volunteered information about their willingness to travel, their intention or otherwise of staying in the industry and their opinion of the management.

Interviewees were assured that any information they gave would not be communicated in any form that would identify an individual source. They were also told both collectively and individually at the beginning of each interview that this inquiry was not initiated by the company but was a piece of independent research. It seems likely that the men were fairly sceptical about this. Nearly all Indian, Pakistani and West Indian interviewees thought the interviewer was officially connected in some way with the company, and usually at some point during the interview produced an individual complaint or request about some detail of company policy. It seems likely that the interviewer has remained in their minds as some ill-defined part of the company's welfare service. The English and Irish interviewees, while probably for the most part without belief in the concept of independent enquiries, were sufficiently confident to talk freely.

Of all interviewees 32 per cent were over 40 years, and 68 per cent were under 40, which shows an average markedly younger than the average adult labour force in other industries. This is predominantly a young man's industry and this no doubt also greatly influences the high mobility rates. Two-thirds were married and living with their families. Of those who had been married, 73 per cent (273) had dependent children (under 15 years), and over half owned their own houses or had council house tenancies. Many of the rest were saving hard to acquire their own homes. This does something to dispel the illusion that building sites are largely manned by undomesticated drifters whose high earnings are all quickly dissipated in the pubs and the betting shop. (There are, of course, some men who do fit this stereotype, but the interviewer encountered only five.)

The interviews were directed primarily at finding out whether stable employment was something that operatives wanted, since, if it were not, the company's aims were perhaps misdirected. 'Do you want stable employment?' is obviously a blunderbuss question to ask directly, and although this question was asked initially, the answers were considered together with much other information collected from and about the interviewees.

Attitudes to stable employment

A large majority (77 per cent) of all interviewees stated that they preferred to remain with one employer, but later qualifications attached to the statement, as well as individual work histories, made it clear that for most of that 77 per cent the answer should have been 'Yes, I prefer to remain with one employer, other things being equal'. The figure of 77 per cent is in direct contradiction to the rates of voluntary turnover actually taking place on the four sites which ranged up to 400–500 with correspondingly low rates of stability. Questions to 360 interviewees (11 apprentices are excluded for this purpose since they were bound by indentures to one employer) revealed that only 26 per cent (95 men) had remained in the company's employ for more than three years (this figure is confirmed from company records); 59 per cent (211 men) told the interviewer they had changed employers between one and three times in the same period; and the remaining 15 per cent had changed employers more than three times. From subsequent enquiries it seems likely that some interviewees underestimated their number of job changes, either through forgetting a site on which they had spent only the odd week, or because they felt that to admit to a very high number of job changes made them sound like unsatisfactory workers. Now if 77 per cent of the interviewees were also sincere in their statement that they preferred to stay with one employer, and if the great bulk of interviewees were not men for whom change is a psychological necessity, what are the factors causing the amount of job change engaged in by operatives in this sector of the construction industry?

74

First it must be emphasized that operatives understand very well the nature of their industry and the problems of an individual employer in the industry. They know that no matter what the employer's intentions are, if the company is engaged in primary construction it cannot promise its employees a lifetime's work in an area convenient to them. They know very well that when a site is coming to an end their employer will have to pay them off, and that even if the company offers them a transfer to the next company site it may be awkwardly located for them. Nearly every interviewee when discussing his own work history pointed out that the situation of operatives in the construction industry is *totally different* from that of operatives in nearly any other industry, e.g. men do not feel any stigma attached to dismissal. An operative in the construction industry, even if he is offered long-term security, as with this particular company investigated, gains it upon conditions which are quite different from most manual workers. In order to take advantage of the company's offer, a man will almost certainly have to live away from home sometimes, or may have to move house and at best must often accept a long journey to work.

If long-term security of employment comes, as it must in primary construction, with these kinds of conditions attached to it, then it is likely to be something that on balance not every man wants. All interviewees were asked whether they were prepared sometimes to live away from home on a job, and 40 per cent (147 men) said that they were, leaving 60 per cent who were not prepared to do so. Any man who said that he did not much like living away from home but would if the job was worth it, was put in the category of men prepared to travel. The remaining 60 per cent were quite definite that they were not prepared to work away from home. Interviewees were asked how long it took them to get to work every day, as a measure of the length of journey operatives were in fact accepting, which may be construed as an indication of the length of journey which operatives would tolerate. Forty-six per cent (172 men) had journeys of half an hour or less, 37 per cent (137 men) between thirty minutes and one hour and only 17 per cent (sixty-two men) were travelling more than an hour. Of these sixty-two were travelling over the hour, a high percentage were plant operatives (who travel with their equipment), older men and coloured immigrants who had more limited job opportunities. It seems it would be fair to say that in general an hour's travel to work is about the top limit for operatives, and one company is unlikely always to be able to provide continuous work within that travelling time for all its employees.

Taken together these facts imply that the candidates for long-term security must be limited to the 40 per cent of interviewees who were prepared to live away from home and perhaps about 17 per cent who had accepted journeys of more than one hour (these two groups overlap somewhat so that the true total proportion is 50 per cent, not 57 per cent). However, a statement that 40 per cent of interviewees were prepared to live away from home and a further 10 per cent were prepared to accept journeys of over one hour to work does not indicate that this is what these operatives *preferred* to do. The Phelps Brown[1] enquiry reports a lower percentage of operatives prepared to live away from home, viz. 33 per cent.

So far it is possible to say definitely that for 50 per cent of the interviewees the conditions on which long-term stability was offered were unacceptable, so that the possibility of long-term security with one employer is not one which they took into account when deciding to take or keep a job. For the other 50 per cent the conditions seemed to be tolerable, but not necessarily what they would choose for themselves, and may have from time to time become intolerable. It follows that for the 50 per cent who would not live away from home and did not accept long journeys, security cannot lie in staying with one employer. It can, therefore, only be in high weekly earnings. The same is true for the 50 per cent prepared to travel and tolerate long journeys, if they had any doubts as to whether they would always want to continue in this pattern.

In this context it must also be remembered that operatives are manual workers whose earnings capacity, being very directly related to their physical condition, tends to decline rather than increase with age. Immediate money earnings are always important to a manual worker who cannot rely, as a professional man or executive does, on his earnings rising with promotion and service throughout his working life. High money earnings are doubly important to a manual worker in an industry like construction where it is the only alternative source of security to the company's offer which comes, through no fault of the company's, with what may be unacceptable conditions attached. As discussed earlier the earnings vary widely between site and site and if other employees could go 'down the road' to the next firm and get a rise of 20 per cent between Friday and Monday, the quit rate from other occupations might well be nearer to the quit rate from building sites.

These three factors—viz. that the particular men under consideration are manual workers whose earnings will decrease rather than increase with age, that long-term stability with one employer requires the acceptance of inconvenient travelling, and that the money

[1] The Phelps Brown *Report*, para. 196, p. 70.

received can vary site by site so greatly go far to explain operatives' preoccupation with bonus-chasing. All interviewees were asked their main reason for entering the construction industry and 344 (92.9 per cent) gave the money that could be earned as a prime reason, although a preference for an open-air life and a varied job was stated as an important factor by 60 per cent of the interviewees. It became clear in the early stages of the enquiry that groups of men could be distinguished as being more or less highly money-motivated. This is *not* to say that any one of these groups is not money-motivated at all, but simply that for some men other factors were sufficiently important to them to be weighed against higher earnings.

It was possible to assess attitudes to stability for only 319 of the 371 interviewees. While the fifty-two interviewees on Site 1 provided valuable information on other points, and contributed to an understanding of money motivation, they were not asked the same questions in the same way and so their answers are not included for this purpose.

There seems to exist a distinguishable group of men who wanted long-term stable employment. They stated in answer to direct questions that they wanted to stay with one employer and that they were not prepared to change jobs just for the money. They answered 'Yes' to the question 'Would you be prepared to stay with one employer to collect redundancy payments?' It was felt that employees' answers to this question were definitive. The money that can be earned varies so greatly on different sites that a man who sticks to one employer may be losing more financially than any redundancy payment could compensate, and the men were aware of this. Operatives also recognized that the Act to some extent commits employers and may preclude them from discharging men with two years' service. It seemed reasonable to assume that an operative prepared to stay to qualify for redundancy payments is prepared to commit himself in order that an employer may be committed to him and is, in short, a man looking for stable employment. Ninety-one men out of 371 answered 'Yes' to this question. Four men did not in the interviewer's opinion sufficiently understand the question, but their answers to other questions placed them in this group. All were Sikhs on Site 2 and all made it quite clear that their prime objective was to be transferred to the next company site and to be allowed to settle down with the company. They have, therefore, been included in this 'stable' group, hereinafter referred to as 'Group 1', which consists of ninety-five men (31 per cent of the total).

The next readily distinguishable group are the men strongly motivated towards the top money, men who do not greatly mind

77

whom they work for, what hours or how hard, provided the money is good. Variously known as 'cowboys', 'high flyers', etc., these men may survive one week of an unusually low pay packet but not two. They are totally uninterested in long-term stability; 14 per cent (forty-six men) fell into this group, which is hereafter called 'Group 3'.

The remaining 55 per cent (178 men) cannot really be further divided. These are not highly mobile men, since they will stay for some time on a site where they are not making their top money; but they are not committed to the idea of stable employment with one employer. This group, referred to hereafter as 'Group 2', contains some men who were once 'high flyers' and may be again, as well as some men who may just be coming round to settling with one company, but it was felt that any further sub-division would be too subjective to be useful.

This division into groups, was made by accepting the men's stated aspirations except where they conflicted directly with information acquired from the company. This conflict occurred in only a few cases between Groups 2 and 3. The statements of a few men would have placed them with the 'high flyers' of Group 3 while the record showed them to have been on a site for a year through very variable pay and times. They were, therefore, included in Group 2. Aspiration by no means always matches reality; men with Group 1 aspirations may never have more than a year with any company because they were not rated worth a transfer. Many men in Group 2 have had several years' service with the company but without being in any way explicitly committed to the idea of staying indefinitely.

Likely factors that might influence operatives' degree of money orientation and interest in stable employment were analysed[1] but it emerged that domestic circumstances, such as marital status and number of dependent children, etc., seemed to have no consistent effect on the degree of money orientation except that the mobile Group 3 includes as would be expected about 10 per cent more single men.

There is perhaps some indication that home ownership is associated with stability inasmuch as the lowest percentage of people with their own house is among the highly mobile men in Group 3. Whether this indicates that home ownership is an expression of the stable employee's general preference for a settled and secure life-style, or whether ownership of a house makes a man seek settled employment, could not be determined from these interviews. Nor can we say similarly how far age, temperament or convenience determined the

[1] See *Security of Employment: a study in the Construction Industry*, PEP Broadsheet No. 505, November 1968.

lower proportion of those who were home owners among highly mobile men.

It therefore appears that the company's offer of long-term stability is only truly welcomed by some 31 per cent of a random sample of its operatives, and that the 31 per cent is not explained by their domestic circumstances. Analysis of the sample by age and nationality shows that these are important factors influencing a man's choices (see Tables I and II).

TABLE I: *Interviewees (319) Grouped by Attitudes to Stable Employment and Age*

Type	Men under 40		Men over 40		All	
	%	No.	%	No.	%	No.
Group 1	24	53	42	42	31	95
Group 2	59	129	50	49	55	178
Group 3	17	38	8	8	14	46
Total	100	220	100	99	100	319

Note: The three groups are as defined earlier: Group 1 is positively interested in stable employment with one employer; Group 2 is not always unstable but not committed to the idea of stability with one employer; Group 3 are not interested in staying with one employer.

As Table I shows, only 24 per cent of the under-40 age-group interviewed appear in Group 1 as truly interested in stability while 42 per cent of the older men appear in this group. Conversely 17 per cent of the younger men are in Group 3 while only 8 per cent of the older men appear in this group.

TABLE II: *Interviewees (319) by Attitudes to Stable Employment and Nationality (per cent)*

Aspiration	Irish	English	Indian and Pakistani	West Indian	Continental European	Others	All
Group 1	18	24	74	61	63	40	31
Group 2	56	63	26	39	37	60	55
Group 3	26	13	—	—	—	—	14
Total	100	100	100	100	100	100	100

This analysis by nationality reveals that only 18 per cent of the Irish interviewees and 24 per cent of native-born interviewees were in Group 1, while 74 per cent of the Indian or Pakistani interviewees,

61 per cent of the West Indians and 63 per cent of the Continental European (mainly Polish and Latvian) interviewees appear in Group 1. Some of the numbers are small and percentages must, therefore, be treated with caution.

Interviews with older men and coloured immigrants suggested that this expressed preference for stability might be because both these groups experienced some difficulty in getting jobs, unlike the other men in the sample. All operatives were asked if they felt confident that they could always get a job. Eleven per cent of the whole sample expressed some doubts, while 33 per cent (20) out of the 60 coloured immigrants felt uncertain. As a group, coloured immigrants were younger than the main sample, 80 per cent of them being under 40 as against 64 per cent of the main sample, so that this lack of confidence is not in their case related to age. Coloured immigrants had had longer periods of unemployment than the main sample.

Men over 40, not coloured immigrants, were not less confident than the rest of the sample that they could get a job, but many felt the life on a primary construction site became very hard for older men. Employment figures suggest that numbers of older men leave primary construction as they get into their fifties. On all sites investigated the overall percentage was that 61 per cent of operatives currently employed were under 40. The Phelps Brown Report found about the same percentage in primary construction. This survey also showed that older men are less in evidence on sites in localities where management has no difficulty recruiting labour. On both Sites 3 and 4 there was some shortage of local employment, and it is significant that Site 3 (the northern housing site) had no operatives over the age of 56 on the site and only 22 per cent of the labour force were over 40. Site 4 (the northern office building contract) had four operatives over 56, all steelfixers, a trade which is in very short supply, and apart from these four only 21 per cent of the labour force were over 40. By contrast at Site 2 (the London suburban building site) which had great difficulty recruiting labour, 38 per cent of its employees were over 40. This would suggest that the older worker is largely a marginal worker, in the sense that his productivity is more likely to slip below the cost of his labour, and that the number of older men employed is mainly a function of the local labour market.

Taken together with Tables I and II which show that a much higher percentage of older men and coloured immigrants want stable employment, these figures suggest that the casual nature of employment in parts of the industry does cause difficulties for the more marginal employees, and that, not unexpectedly, it is these more marginal employees who are seeking stability of employment. A

80

further exercise was conducted to test this hypothesis by extracting those operatives who wanted stability to the point where they were prepared to live away from home if necessary in order to remain stable with one company. This group is referred to as Group 1(a) in Table III below.

TABLE III: *Comparison of Group 1a (42 Men) Interviewees with Groups 1b, 2 and 3 (277) by Age and Nationality*

	Group 1a		Groups 1b, 2 and 3	
	number	per cent	number	per cent
Over 40	19	45	83	30
(of whom those over 56)	(6)	(14)	(15)	(6)
Coloured immigrants	18	43	42	15
Remainder	5	12	152	55
Total	42	100	277	100

This gives a significant picture of the men anxious about stability. Only 31 per cent of all interviewees were considering stability at all, and only 13 per cent, the 42 men in Group 1a, could be said to have had security of employment as an *overriding objective*. It appears, therefore, that operatives' concern with stability relates to their position in the labour market in terms of age and nationality.

It would therefore seem that the company is offering a benefit which 69 per cent of all operatives (assuming that the sample is representative of this section of the industry) do not actively want. A further 18 per cent do not want stability enough to accept the disadvantages of travelling that may go with it so that it could be said that 87 per cent of the sample were men who saw themselves as working within an industry and changing employers from time to time for convenience and higher earnings. They appear to have accepted this as the best way of accommodating themselves to an occupation where employers are forced frequently to change the size, character and location of their labour force, and where, as was found by the Phelps Brown Report, the great majority of men value their freedom to move about from one employer to another.[1]

Conversely, 13 per cent certainly and perhaps all the 31 per cent who wanted stability are not suited by the industry's arrangements and it is perhaps for them that the company's concept of social responsibility is valuable. As part of the survey a cross-analysis was made to estimate how many of this 31 per cent who wanted stability had achieved it with the company. The answer was that less than one-third of them had achieved three years' service with the company.

[1] Para. 235, p. 81.

This makes business sense, as clearly the company would not want a stable labour force entirely composed of older men and (in so far as many of these are still relatively inexperienced workers) immigrants, but does demonstrate that, on the facts, the company's policy of social responsibility is not in fact giving stable employment to the majority of those who most want it.

Of the 31 per cent who do seek stable employment and as such would be beneficiaries of the company's concept of its social responsibility to its employees, only one-third had achieved stability with the company. It seems therefore that in this respect the company's concept of its social responsibilities is benefiting only 10 per cent of its work force and that the company can economically use only one-third of those for whom the policy would be most valuable. To the extent that these interview results are representative, 69 per cent of the primary construction labour force feel they have made the best bargain for themselves in the light of conditions in their industry by opting to work for an *industry*, and that they will work for a *company* only for as long as convenient sites are available. It may be argued that this is hardly a matter of choice for these men but in an era of full employment with many other jobs available which offer security of employment (and some of the men interviewed had worked in other occupations), at any rate for younger men, staying in the construction industry is not an inescapable bondage. Most interviewees stressed that they well understood the nature of their industry and in selecting it had chosen high earnings, variety, change and an open air life in preference to the security offered by a factory industry. The growth of labour-only demonstrates the type of choice often made by operatives in sub-contracting this industry; they are a self-selected group and must be considered as such.

Pension schemes

Of all hourly-paid and works staff, some 2,000 are in the pension scheme out of an hourly-paid labour force of 11,000 to 12,000. Since the qualifying period to enter the scheme for hourly-paid workers is five years' service (two years for key men) and only 3,500 operatives have over two years' service, this figure probably means that effectively everyone eligible for the pension scheme has joined. The scheme provides a payment of 12s per week in the lowest category, and a minimum annual pension of £15 in respect of each complete year of membership of the scheme, as well as standard benefits in the event of a member's death before pensionable age.

From the operative's point of view there are short-comings to what seems like a reasonable and sensible provision. The qualifying period of five years' service is long enough to exclude many potential beneficiaries, but is considered to be the shortest qualifying period possible to avoid excessive administrative costs due to operatives moving in and out of the scheme. However, in manual employment, five years is a fairly long time to have to wait before becoming eligible for a pension scheme.

Another difficulty with the pension scheme is that it operates from 'normal pensionable age', i.e. 65. The Phelps Brown Report and the statistics collected in this survey do indicate that, because of some combination of personal choice and lessening opportunity, operatives tend to leave primary construction for less demanding work (local authority maintenance, for example) in their fifties. The existence of a company pension scheme may induce operatives to remain on heavy work in primary construction rather than, as their family and therefore income needs are reduced, moving into less highly paid but also less physically demanding work.

It seems therefore that the company's provision of a pension scheme may not be the benefit it seems to operatives because it is limited in scope by a long qualifying period, is beginning to clash with state provision and is discouraging older operatives from changing to less strenuous employment.

AMENITIES AND SAFETY

a. *Site amenities*

The company studied makes it clear in its literature that it aims to offer good fringe benefits, a high standard of amenities (canteens, washrooms, etc.) and a high degree of concern for safety. A part of the interviews was directed to find out to what extent operatives were concerned with these factors of their employment. The short answer, firmly given by most men, was that they were not at all concerned, provided the money was right. This is an oversimplification, as became clear when the interviewer postulated an extreme case to interviewees: given a choice between two sites, one where the money was £5 or so better per week but where the only lavatory was half a mile away and there was no canteen, and a site with less money but standard company amenities, which would they choose? Even so, about 50 per cent of all interviewees opted for the former site with the extra £5 a week, but the others agreed that if the sum involved was only £1 or so a week they would choose a site with good amenities.

However, most interviewees pointed out that all sites operated by large construction companies these days had a reasonable level of amenities (these are required by statute and by Working Rule

Agreements), so that the real choice they had was between slightly different standards of amenities. It became absolutely clear that provided that the basic amenities are available, men take little account of marginal differences in choosing where to work. A well-known smaller company provides showers for the men and several interviewees spoke of these with admiration but proved on investigation to have deserted the showers for a somewhat higher bonus on a less well-endowed site. With this overall reservation an analysis was made of those men who felt that amenities were totally unimportant. Interestingly 18 per cent of the younger men, while not caring about canteens, felt washrooms were important, as against only 9 per cent of the older men, and this may be related to generational differences about willingness to go home dirty from work.

The company's provision of amenities such as paid travelling time, boots and donkey jackets was similarly discounted by most men. It is not that the company's provision was unappreciated, but that *all* national companies make similar provision.

b. Safety

The company's preoccupation with safety was recognized and appreciated by operatives, but for very few of them was this a matter of direct concern. Overall 11 per cent of all interviewees (but 25 per cent of all interviewees on the civil engineering site) felt any serious concern with the level of safety precautions on a site. Again it is not that the company's concern goes unnoticed; simply that all national companies are fairly well alerted about safety in this particularly dangerous industry.

None of this evidence indicates that the company's provision of better amenities and its concern for safety does not benefit its operatives: clearly it does. It does suggest however that operatives are much more concerned with a good pay packet than marginally better site amenities, and the latter will not provide an overriding reason for staying with one company if better bonus is to be earned with another.

BENEFITS TO THE COMPANY ACCRUING FROM THE COMPANY'S CONCEPT OF SOCIAL RESPONSIBILITY

b. Stability of employment

From the company's financial point of view the offer of stable employment arises from the need to attract and hold reliable stable labour to man its contracts. What a company in primary construction wants from its labour force is contract stability, i.e. they want some employees to be prepared to come on site in the early difficult stages and to stay throughout a contract as long as they are needed. In the company studied, in part the offer of long-term stability to some men is to ensure that there is an adequate labour force which will be stable throughout a contract. To some extent the company's transfer policy serves this end but there is still a disruptively high rate of turnover on many contracts. Overall, it appears that this company is not in a markedly better position than that of other large companies whose policy is to keep only foremen and dismiss all other operatives at the end of a contract, engaging labour again as and where required for the next undertaking. Turnover *per se* may not matter if it is confined to a certain part of the labour force. A site with a high turnover and low stability will be in trouble; a site with high turnover and high stability may not be. An examination of the records of the four sites makes this clear.

For example, Site 2 (the large municipal housing estate near London) had great difficulty at all stages of the contract in getting and keeping suitable labour and the high labour-turnover rate severely affected productivity. Turnover (annual average) in the early stages of the contract was 339 per cent overall, 234 per cent in the middle stages and 126 per cent as the contract drew to a close. (Turnover figures were slightly lower, but not much, among the Sikh employees on the contract.) The dismissal rate was exceptionally low, about 11 per cent of all pay-offs. The turnover rate *per se* did not explain the contract's difficulties since high rates of turnover were found in two contracts where no difficulty with labour recruitment was experienced. It is the stability rate which proves to be crucial to work organization. It was not possible to compare directly annual stability rates for the four contracts studied since Site 2 had been running for over two years when interviews were conducted, Site 3 for eight months, Site 4 for five months, and Site 5 for just over a year, but a comparison can be made by comparing percentages of men employed on the contract from the beginning who had been stable throughout. These rates are calculated historically, i.e. they are men who started on site during the first six months and were either still there at the time of interviewing, or in the case of Site 2 had been paid off before interviews started but had served over a year on the site before leaving.

Table IV indicates the relationship prevailing between stability and labour turnover. On Site 4, which had easily the highest rate of turnover, this turnover was confined to 47 per cent of the labour force and in fact the site had no trouble recruiting and keeping the labour it wanted. Much of its turnover was a function of a high dismissal rate and transfers, i.e. transferred men who demanded within one day to be returned to their site of origin. Site 3 with a turnover confined mainly to only 35 per cent of its operatives felt they had no special problems with labour. Site 5, whose turnover was the lowest but which also had a low stability rate, felt they were not so fortunately placed and reported difficulties. Site 2, with the same low stability percentage as Site 5 but a much higher turnover rate, encountered great difficulties in getting their contract started at all and felt productivity was seriously impaired by their labour problems.

TABLE IV: *Comparison of Rates of Labour Turnover and Labour Stability at the End of the First Six Months on Sites 2–5*

Site	Annual average turnover (per cent)	Labour strength	Number of stable men	Percentage of stable men	Overall percentage of pay-offs dismissed
Site 2	354	210	77	37	10
Site 3	240	46	30	65	36
Site 4	473	60	32	53	23
Site 5	218	294	110	37	26

Notes: (i) Figures for Site 2 do not include any Sikh operatives since no Sikh operatives were started in the first six months of this contract.

(ii) Figures for percentages dismissed are overall for the whole course of the contract except for Site 4 which had only been running for six months.

These figures suggest, and subsequent research undertaken by the company goes some way to confirm, that if a site can achieve 50 per cent stability rate, i.e. can confine the turnover to only half of its labour force, then the site can tolerate almost any amount of turnover in that half.

However, even given the empirical evidence which suggests that labour turnover may not be as serious in its effects as the rates would indicate, it is the combination of high turnover and low stability that makes a site especially difficult to run. This is particularly obvious from companies' difficulties in getting contracts started. This problem is of major concern to the company studied and provides the main justification given for the economic value of their policy of stabilizing some men with the company. Their aim is to stabilize some men over the long term to have available a stable force that will settle at the beginning of contracts and be quickly productive. Figures for the turnover rate of men transferred on to the four sites investigated show that, at least from the point of view of reducing turnover, this policy is effective.

TABLE V: *Annual Average Turnover Percentages for Transferred Men and New Hirings on Sites 2–5 (per cent)*

State of contract labour force	Site 2			Site 3		Site 4		Site 5	
	Sikhs	Non-Sikhs							
	New hirings	New hirings	Trans-ferred	New hirings	Trans-ferred	New hirings	Trans-ferred	New hirings	Trans-ferred
Building up to peak	697	392	71	382	30	660	203	305	62
Peak	134	292	63	271	77	*	*	208	57
Running down	124	202	53	*	*	*	*	*	*

* Not available.

Note: Only six Sikh operatives were transferred so figures are not separated.

87

The table shows that turnover is very substantially lower among transferred operatives than new hirings, but it is still, by the standards of other industries, fairly high, even among the more stable men. Even so, the transfer policy is definitely contributing to lessened turnover.

The preliminary conclusion would then be that the transfer policy is useful. However, there are problems. First, the company has been operating this policy for a long time and they still have only about 27 per cent stable operatives (i.e. men who have been with them for over two years). It looks as if 27 per cent stability rate is not high enough since Site 2, which had 37 per cent stability, was in serious difficulties at the start of its contract. Moreover, the distribution of this 27 per cent is not even. Table VI shows the differences in the percentages of transferred men on the four sites. (Not all of these men have had two years' service with the company, which explains why the percentages seem high in relation to 27 per cent of all company operatives with over two years' service.)

TABLE VI: *Current Labour Force of Sites 2–5 at the Time Data Collected by Transferred Men and New Hirings (per cent)*

	Site 2		Site 3	Site 4	Site 5
	Sikhs	Others			
Transfers	7	28	44	43	30
New hirings	93	72	56	57	70

Sites 2 and 5 were both London sites, where stability tends to be low and turnover rates tend to be very high as a function of the labour market. On these two sites the company had a much lower percentage of transferred men, whereas on the two northern sites, where it is much easier to recruit labour, the company had high percentages of transferred men. To be effective the company's stable labour should have counteracted the state of the local labour market, but transferred men do not appear to have been used in this way.

In addition to this problem of maldistribution (whose existence has been confirmed by subsequent research done for the company) it also seemed likely that transferring operatives might be expensive for the company.

It seems that the company can readily increase its stable labour force of those who would be willing to travel to the places where the company needs them, only by recruiting more of the Group 1 security-minded operatives, and this may not be the most effective policy (see, survey results). Building up a stable labour force is an expensive business since operatives acquire expensive service-related claims against the company and some immunity from dismissal, which may mean that men who become unsatisfactory will be frequently transferred from site to site. The stable labour force in the company was older than the average, nearly 50 per cent more than forty years old against the average of 38 per cent.

Subsequent research undertaken by the company into the cost-effectiveness of a large sample of their operatives reveals that, while the 41–56 year old age group are as cost-effective as the 31–40 age group, and more cost-effective than the under 30 group, the over 56-year-old group is markedly less cost-effective. It is of course likely that one result of a policy of offering stable employment, together with pensions that operatives cannot draw until they are in their sixties, will be that men over 56 will stay with the company, rather than, following the trend noted by the Phelps Brown Report, leave for less demanding work.

Similarly, 'travelling men' in the company, i.e. long-service operatives who will go wherever they are needed, tend to be very expensive labour. Not only must they be paid £5 19s subsistence per week, but it is likely that they generate demands for excessive overtime working. A man living away from his home with nothing much else to do at weekends and evenings, would usually rather earn money than sit idle. This pattern is inevitable in civil engineering because major projects like motorways are not usually near any centre of population, but it may be unnecessarily expensive to use 'travelling men' (as were 15 per cent of the labour on Site 4) for building projects where there is likely to be a local labour force available.

The real problem about a 'travelling man' is that, in order to be worth his £6 travelling pay to the company, he must considerably increase his output. Research done by the company investigated shows that, at various levels of effort, an operative being paid for travelling must produce between 20 and 40 per cent more output than a man not receiving this payment. This is a large increase and it was not surprising that company research revealed that only a minority of travelling men could increase their output by this much.

Obviously on sites where the company has either to make travelling payments or do without labour this calculation is irrelevant. This company, however, has 27 per cent of its labour force to place by transference, and may often find that the only site on which a particular operative can be placed will be one to which he has to travel, necessitating a charge of £5 19s to the site which might well have been able to get an equivalent operative locally at no extra charge.

The pension scheme

There is no evidence that the company's provision of a pension scheme is contributing to increased stability and lowered turnover except among the 31 per cent of operatives who appear to set a high priority on continuous employment with one employer. Presumably, the presence of a pension scheme is for them one of the attractions of continuous employment. On the other hand the company does not seem to want to offer continuous employment to more than about one-third of this group, including as it does substantial numbers of expensive older men and recently-arrived immigrants who may frequently require special training and supervision.

A pension scheme in which benefits start at 65 is moreover helping to keep operatives with the company until that age. In terms of the company's findings that operatives are markedly less cost-effective after the age of 56 this policy is working to the company's detriment, and by keeping older workers in a very heavy occupation not in the interests of employees or of an economic distribution of the labour force. To the extent that firms ought to accept responsibility for the depreciation by age of its labour force in this industry an industry-wide transferable pension scheme would seem to be the best way to reconcile the interests of companies and employees.

By operatives' own statements (see pp. 83–84) the company's provision of amenities, etc., beyond statutory requirements does not much influence their decisions when it comes to changing jobs. From a strictly economic point of view, therefore, the company is not improving its competitive position by this type of additional fringe-benefit expenditure.

CONCLUSIONS

The core of the company's concept of its social responsibilities and the feature which is most relevant to the company's costs and efficiency is the provision of continuous employment. The case-study shows how the provision of long-term stability of employment for more than a minority of workers is, by the nature of the industry, neither economic nor much desired.

The main group for whom security is highly desirable are older men, immigrants and perhaps a few other men with little skill or experience. The company can economically employ some of these men continuously, given their readiness to be transferred from site to site, and they can be provided with benefits related to company service.

There are a number of other aspects of working conditions, such as site amenities, safety enforcement and procedures for preventing arbitrary dismissal which it might be suggested are the social responsibilities of construction companies. To the extent that such conditions are successfully maintained or improved to attract the labour force needed (and the survey suggests that they may be of only limited value in this respect), they are undertaken for good business reasons. To the extent that it is believed that such improvements will attract a better type of labour into the industry as a whole and generally improve industrial relations, these are again good business reasons but, owing to the degree of movement of labour from employer to employer, these would be better dealt with by the industry as a whole, rather than by the individual firms. There is a precedent for the successful organization of industry-wide benefit in the present Holiday Pay Scheme. Pending industry-wide developments, however, it is to be expected that larger companies will give a lead to their industry by pioneering improvements in working conditions and terms of employment. These are more likely to be justifiable on the grounds of good business or social responsibility or both if they are based upon the fullest consultation about what combination of earnings and occupational benefits employees themselves prefer.

Thus, though providing greater stability of employment in a notoriously 'casual' industry would appear at first to be a proper exercise of the social responsibilities of firms in that industry, a closer examination suggests that the interests neither of companies nor of their employees would be served by an undiscriminating extension of stability of employment with individual firms. Companies need to measure, on the basis of accurate costing, the profitability of different levels of labour stability. On these calculations a flexible structure of pay and conditions can be based which will secure the 'contract' stability of labour required from site to site.

The question then arises whether the company should use its resources to finance further stability, beyond what may be required in order to maximize profit. Most employees in the present state of employment are not greatly concerned about job security with one company as long as they gain high earnings, except for a minority group of workers, viz. the elderly, immigrants and the totally unskilled. These men are the most vulnerable group, and it might be argued that they most need socially responsible policies to protect them.

On the other hand, since the industry has the advantage of a mobile labour force which is prepared to belong to an industry rather than one company, there is a strong case for an industry-wide scheme for construction workers of the same kind of occupational benefits as are customarily provided company by company in other industries. Any requirement for improved conditions of employment which might be extended throughout the whole industry must, of course, take account of the very wide range of size of firms and must not place onerous burdens upon very small businesses.

Attempts to improve working conditions must be more directly related than hitherto to the conditions of the industry if they are to be effective. For example, in the case of provision for retirement, pending an industry-wide scheme, a limited company provision added to the state pension would not be as attractive, bearing in mind tax liability, as the offer of a uniform lump-sum severance payment from fifty-five years onwards. This would enable men to leave the industry for lighter work and the company to shed older, less productive labour and thus to reconcile the interests of both. It would likewise be much more beneficial for firms to pursue an active redeployment policy for men around that age, i.e. to help them get more suitable jobs in, say, secondary construction, than to subsidize their retention on primary construction sites.

The reasons why this company pursued a policy of trying to stabilize a greater part of its labour force were mixed. In part it was done for what were thought to be good business reasons, i.e. creating a more stable labour force attached to the company over the long term, and having a name for being a good employer on the grounds that this is a valuable recruiting asset (though this is likely to be far less significant in industries where most men are not committing themselves to permanent employment); and partly it was done because the company believed it was a better way to treat its labour force. In the event, the policies adopted did not succeed in certain important respects. The company did not achieve markedly lower turnover or higher stability rates than its competitors, the provision of amenities seemed to be of only secondary significance to its employees, and only about one-third of its labour force appeared to rate job-security as the most important characteristic of their employment. The high cost of keeping and transferring employees was subsequently verified by the company's own intensive studies of labour costs. In short, the policy failed to improve the use of the company's labour resources from the economic or financial point of view. It was more successful in bringing social benefits to certain of the operatives, though here it may be strongly argued that the money should have been better spent, from the point of view both of the men's welfare and of economic efficiency, on a policy aimed at enabling the older men to get less exacting jobs in other sectors.

The construction firm in which this study was made is a close company controlled by a family whose members have been outstanding in public service and in giving leadership in their industry. By the criterion of operating profits as a percentage of capital employed and as a percentage of turnover, this company, though high in size of capital employed, stands low in the list of large construction companies. Clearly its directors set a high value on social responsibility to their employees, when they invested resources of effort and money in their policy for stabilizing employment. But careful measurement and analysis indicate that not only was this policy unprofitable, but it also failed to provide for the employees in the way that would meet their needs. The lesson would seem to be that companies' social policies as well as their straight business operations should be based on careful measurement and analysis. The company in our case study has, as it happens, in fact undertaken such a review and as a result revised its policy.

Chapter 4

Case Study III: Company Giving

The amounts given by individual companies are, in relation to their assets and income, quite small, being on average 0.54 per cent of net company incomes. But to invest even a small part of a company's resources in activities which are not apparently intended to contribute to the efficiency and profitability of that company would seem, from the point of view of the existing company law in Britain, to require justification. To the extent that the explanation is based upon the idea that a business firm has obligations to the community, both immediate and wider, in which it operates, the reasons why company boards make donations, and support one rather than another type of charitable effort, throw some light on a company's concept of its social responsibilities.

Company subscriptions to charities and the arts have become a widespread and accepted business practice. The duty of company boards to exercise their powers in the best interests of the shareholders is not held to exclude them from making such donations, and this view has not been challenged in the courts since 1921 (*Evans* v. *Brunner Mond & Co. Ltd.* [1921] I, Ch. 359). Some companies have included in their Articles of Association an objects clause which specifically empowers the company to make donations. Unilever, for example, has an objects clause which enables it to subscribe or guarantee money for charitable, religious, scientific, educational and benevolent objects, and generally for any public or useful object. Other companies feel this is unnecessary as their donations are unlikely to be challenged, and if they were it would not be difficult to defend them as being broadly consistent with the long-term interests of the company and its shareholders. In strict law it is of course not sufficient for a company to have a power to make charitable donations, it must also be able to show that these are beneficial to the company's interest. The Jenkins Committee concluded that 'the practice which has developed, of companies (without express powers) making donations to general charities of no direct interest to the company's business has never been challenged in the courts of this country and we venture to think that this practice, which is regarded

94

by businessmen as necessary to create or preserve goodwill for their companies would, on that ground, be acceptable to the courts today'.[1]

For American companies the law is clearer on this point. In the United States the legality of corporation gifts was deliberately put to the test in 1954 in the case of a gift by A. P. Smith Manufacturing to the University of Princeton. The New Jersey Supreme Court not only allowed this expenditure, but handed down a judgement which positively encouraged corporation giving: 'Corporate contributions . . . to Princeton and institutions rendering the like public service, are, if held within reasonable limitations, a matter of direct benefit to the giving corporations . . . it may well be regarded as a major, though unwritten, corporate power and in the court's view it is a solemn duty' (Judge Alfred A. Stein). In most state jurisdictions in the United States a company does not have to justify a gift as showing any direct benefit to the company.

Although, in general, doubts about the legality of their actions do not cause companies in Britain to refrain from making gifts, the lack of a clear rationale and the uncertainties which some boards feel about their actions in this respect are probably reflected in the strict limits set by some companies both to the amounts given and to the purposes to which they are devoted. If company boards feel unsure of the place charitable giving has in business enterprise, they may restrict their gifts to modest sums and non-controversial causes.

More important in determining the level of company donations is the extent to which they are tax deductible. Some expenditure very directly related to a company's business, such as specialized technical training or research, may be held to be 'in furtherance of trade' and allowable as business expenses, but such expenditure is very closely scrutinized for tax deduction. The greater part of company expenditure on education, research, social welfare and the arts is in the form of donations given under covenants which do not bear corporation tax. Section 52 (4) of the Finance Act 1965 relieves covenanted donations (for any period capable of exceeding six years) by corporate bodies to charities of corporation tax (now 42½ per cent) thus enabling a company to make a donation the net cost of which is substantially less than the gross amount covenanted. Deeds of covenant are widely used by companies for payments directly to charities or to the Charities Aid Fund (itself a discretionary trust) or in some circumstances to transfer payments to separate company trusts or foundations.

The American system whereby up to 5 per cent of companies' pre-

[1] *Company Law Committee Report*, Cmnd. 1749, HMSO, 1962.

tax income is tax deductible if devoted to charities is often held to be a more positive incentive to corporate philanthropy, although the power to give up to 5 per cent is not exercised by most American companies and amounts given by them rarely exceed 1 per cent (up to 1961 aggregate company contributions exceeded 1 per cent of pre-tax income in only three years).[1]

The tax treatment of charitable contributions varies considerably in Europe.[2] For example, in Austria, Belgium, Finland and Sweden, as in the United Kingdom, gifts to charities are not deductible from corporate income tax, though Sweden allows gifts to be deductible as business expenses if they are directed to causes which have a close connection with the donor's business or are of direct benefit to the company's employees. Denmark permits tax deduction on corporate income transferred for at least ten years, and Norway allows up to 10 per cent deduction for contributions to institutions concerned with scientific research and vocational and professional education. In France, corporate gifts are deductible only up to 0.5 per cent of company income in general and up to a further 0.2 per cent for gifts to approved scientific and research institutions. Dutch fiscal concessions are more generous, for gifts are deductible from taxable income up to 3 per cent of profits; but the most liberal tax incentives are given in Germany where general charitable gifts are deductible up to 5 per cent and contributions solely for scientific purposes are deductible up to 10 per cent of taxable income. Companies in Europe as in America do not give up to the limits of fiscal concessions; in Germany for example corporations use only about 1 per cent of the 5 per cent deductions which could be claimed.

Strictly considered, the use of covenants by British companies involves their boards in some contradictory policies. On the one hand, a covenant to charity should have in it an element of public benefit but must confer no benefit upon the donor nor must the donor attach counter stipulations or conditions to his gift. On the other hand, companies may find themselves justifying the sums they have covenanted to charities as conferring some discernible benefits upon the company and its shareholders.

To examine more closely how boards dealt with these apparent contradictions, the policies of four companies were explored in some detail and enquiries made among another much larger group of companies.

---

[1] Orace Johnson, 'Corporate Philanthropy', *Journal of Business*, University of Chicago, October 1966.

[2] George Nebolsine, *Fiscal Aspects of Foundations and Charitable Donations in European Countries*, The European Cultural Foundation.

Three large companies' donations policies

Company A is a large international group of over 500 companies. Its size and resources make it an object of first resort for charitable appeals. To discharge what it feels to be its responsibilities and at the same time to meet what might otherwise be an intolerable pressure on the chairman and board members, the group has published a considered statement of its policy for grants to non-profit-making activities, and has a formal machinery for dealing with appeals. The policy for the United Kingdom is very different from that evolved by the group's companies in North and South America, in Africa and the Far East.

In the United Kingdom, operating companies decide on their own donations in the light of their business connections and local needs, but they would not be likely to make a grant exceeding £1,000 without consulting the headquarters of the international company which is responsible for the bulk of philanthropic payments. All appeals are referred to a grants committee which consists of one senior director, and four or five other members appointed for their personal experience or special knowledge, e.g. a scientist who can judge and assess advice on appeals for scientific research, together with a full-time paid secretary. Appeals are judged by their relevance to the company's concept of its responsibilities, and where 'the placing of grants will best foster initiative and attract the support of others'. These considerations have been interpreted to include education, to which twice as much is given as to all other objects, with special reference to science and technology. Projects with international connections and some medical charities are also considered sympathetically. The company does not believe it has a charter for general philanthropy and, except in special circumstances, it does not give to religious denominations, sports, hospitals, charities for social welfare, orchestras, theatres or ballet, individual schools and colleges or purely local causes. It has given on the other hand to funds and activities concerned with overseas students, Voluntary Service Overseas, and campaigns for 'Freedom from Hunger' and 'Feed the Minds', and to the World Wild Life Fund, etc., because of the international connections of these causes. It has made substantial contributions to medical research through medical charities and professional bodies. The company's gifts have however, been mainly concentrated on higher education and research and have amounted to over £1 million in the UK in grants for educational purposes (excluding research grants). The group has also helped schools by contributing to the Industrial Fund,[1]

---

[1] See below.

to developments in teaching mathematics in schools and to many projects designed to interest young people in science and technology. The group is prepared to give continuing interest and support as well as money to the causes it espouses.

The group's companies in the United States have accepted the current business attitudes to philanthropy there, viz. that it is undoubtedly one of the social responsibilities of industry. A Companies Foundation was established in 1953 and in the following ten years gave over £3.4 million for charitable, health, educational, religious, or literary purposes. The Foundation makes grants to local causes and communities in which the company's employees live and work, and in its first ten years one-third of its grants were to community chests, united funds and similar joint community efforts. The Foundation has also continued the companies' earlier policies of financing fellowships and scholarships with special reference to science and mathematics.

The group's companies in other areas operating through foundations and by direct company grants have found it appropriate to finance agricultural research, the building of housing and hospitals and schools. Thus, though there are some common themes, e.g. refusal to support any party political causes and orientation to scientific and technological education, which run through all of the group's non-profit-making grants, a group of companies of this size and geographical spread has to leave its members free to adapt donative policies to local needs and conditions. In the UK the concentration of large donations on education, research, and international causes is justified by the company as enhancing the prestige and serving the business needs of the group to the ultimate benefit of the shareholders.

Company B is also a large international company with subsidiaries and associated companies both in the UK and overseas. The full amount of local giving overseas varies considerably from year to year according to circumstances, e.g. the creation of a local disaster fund, but local giving by associated companies in the UK is usually small and all bigger appeals are dealt with by the parent company.

The policy of the company is generally to respond to selected national appeals not local causes, or alternatively to give grants to national societies which will be responsible for allocating grants to their own local groups. In the latter case the company may specify that the money be allocated in relatively small amounts, e.g. £75 or less. This saves the company time, and avoids the making of invidious choices, but spreads the company's gifts widely.

Charitable appeals are divided by this company into general social welfare (the needs of old people, children, the disabled, etc.) and education and research. The company has a clause in its objects which enables it to give moneys for charitable purposes, but establishing that such moneys are spent to the benefit of the shareholders is of course another matter. Expenditure on education and research, which is more that £130,000 per year, is felt by the Board to be easily defended on grounds of business as well as public interest, e.g. recruiting future staff with appropriate education and skills and sponsoring relevant research, etc. In the field of social welfare, individual items, especially small sums given to particular charities, are however defended solely on the grounds of their cumulative effect in producing goodwill and a good public image for the company. At the least it is believed that a failure to respond to such appeals might be harmful to the company since company donations are now generally expected.

The company has two Appeals Committees, one for education and one for 'benevolent charities', with four directors and the company secretary on each committee. The committee secretary sifts appeals and sends forward those which seem to be within the company's policy for grant-making with suggestions for possible action and amounts which may be appropriate. The secretary can consult other people in the company organization, e.g. the company medical staff, about the appeals of medical charities. The secretary may also consult the secretary of an independent trust whose assets are in the company's shares, since it was set up out of the personal fortune of a former chairman and has some of the present board members as its trustees, but which functions completely separately as an independent trust. Consultation is to avoid duplication in response to appeals.

Appeals which will in general not be considered by this company are those for:

denominational religious bodies (except possibly the preservation of historic buildings);
the arts generally;
local causes;
international charities (associated companies will give in the countries in which they are located).

The chairman and other senior members of the company try to avoid being involved in committees sponsoring charities and do not approve of involving their employees in charitable gifts, e.g. they do not offer to match what employees give. This, which is a common practice in the United States, is disapproved of by this company as

99

exerting undue influence on employees, who should be free to give or not as they decide.[1]

The committees work to budgets, and charitable gifts for social welfare are channelled through the Charities Aid Fund.[2] An excess expenditure in one year due to the need to contribute to some unforeseen national appeal is acceptable, but any persistent overspending would be quickly checked by the board. Political donations have never been made from this company's funds.

The company accepts that it has become an expected obligation of companies to make donations and considers that large companies have to give a lead. It tries to give at about the level of other big companies and would certainly not wish to fall below them. The use of a formal machinery and a budget for appeals provides some protection against pressure, but does not prevent its policy being operated flexibly. On one occasion it informed its shareholders about its donations policy and the amounts disbursed, though this appeared to arouse virtually no interest among them! Senior people in this company candidly admit that considerations of obtaining favourable publicity, pleasing customers, and keeping up with other leading companies for the least possible outlay are factors which can influence its donations policy. They believe that these are legitimate business considerations to apply to spending the shareholders' money.

This attitude of 'cool self-interest' as it has been described in this company has not prevented it from offering without being asked, very large gifts to university education and the company is one of the ten or twelve companies whose support is sought by all fund raisers before they feel secure in launching any sizeable national appeal.

Company C is a large company but well below Companies A and B in size. Its main market is in the British Isles, but it both exports and produces overseas. Members of the Board of this company firmly believe that industry does have social responsibilities, that it ought to try to act as a good citizen in the localities in which it

[1] The practice of companies matching employees' gifts does not necessarily involve any pressure on employees to contribute. Some British companies believe that there are cogent arguments in favour of matching the gifts of their employees. The company giving is used to stimulate generosity in others and to counteract a tendency for individuals to leave gifts to industry because they think their contributions are insignificant. Matching money raised by employees with a company contribution brings all interests in the company—employees, shareholders and management—into consideration of charitable contributions.

[2] The Charities Aid Fund is a discretionary trust with which companies can covenant a sum which can then be allocated on their instructions, thus enabling all their gifts to benefit the donees fully since they can recover tax.

operates, and that its donative policies do not have to be justified as being undertaken for exclusively business reasons. Its board approves an annual budget for donations after a careful review of the previous year's expenditure, and allows an unallocated sum to meet new appeals which may commend themselves later. The company uses the Charities Aid Fund as a vehicle for its donations and, where appropriate, seeks the advice of the National Council of Social Service about the relative merits of different charities. The company believes that charitable giving is a commitment to interest in the objects supported and not just the price of peace, and its chairman, managing director and other board members hold office in a number of local and national charities. Company staff are encouraged to take part in voluntary and statutory service and can be released during working hours for this purpose.

Annual donations, which amount to about £138,000 (about 0.22 per cent of capital employed and 1 per cent of net income), are divided between:

Social welfare	7 per cent
Recreation, public amenities, and the arts	12 per cent
Education and training	37 per cent
Research	40 per cent
Miscellaneous	4 per cent

This company, like Companies A and B, is one of the group of companies whose support and approval would be sought before any sizeable national appeal was launched.

The board of course takes into account in making its decisions the effect that these will have on the company's public image, and its prestige in the business community. Its members believe that a reasonable amount of enlightened philanthropy is a good business investment, but they do not undertake it for that reason. The company holds that business generally, and the leading firms in particular, should accept charitable giving as part of their responsibilities to the community.

These three companies illustrate some of the ways in which donative policies are related to a company's general policy and its peculiar trading position. All three companies are large, well known, and sell branded products which are household names directly to the consumer. They have to be very sensitive about their reputation with the general public. All have associated companies operating overseas and have experience of the importance of making their commercial activities socially acceptable in alien cultures. Two of the three have operated in areas where 'the company' was initially the source of almost all employment, social welfare and education, and they are accustomed to weighing the immediate and longer-term business returns on this kind of social investment and also to erecting some defences against political pressures. All of the firms either as individual companies or as part of an industry have had recent experience of being the object of criticism from the Monopolies Commission or the Prices and Incomes Board (with reference to tied outlets, market share, etc.) and these aspects of their trading position must have some influence upon their concept of 'social responsibilities'.

Companies A and B are quite clear that non-profit-seeking activities must be justified as part of an overall business strategy. Company A states it 'exists for business reasons and has no charter to dispense charity for charity's sake. Relevance to its own responsibilities . . . is equally important with the intrinsic worth of an appeal' (company statement of policy for grant making).

Company B remarks: 'Ironically, the only motive that justifies a company giving money to a charity is one that would be the least meritorious of all in the private individual—cool self-interest. Logically, therefore, the amount given should be the minimum necessary to achieve the purpose of preserving the good name and reputation of the company' (company spokesman).

Company C is not unmindful of the business pay-off from its benefactions to charity but is more concerned with the merits of appeals from the community's point of view than from its own. While the top executives of Company B deliberately try not to become too involved with the charities they support, the board and senior staff of Company C believe they must give service and interest as well as money to causes of which they approve. This is largely a personal rather than a company matter and it is inevitable that highly subjective decisions will be made about company donations as about individual ones, even when processed through the machinery of appeals committees. To which it should be added that individuals as well as companies have mixed motives, some of them unlovely, for charitable giving.

A very important difference between the first two companies and the third, and one which may be most significant in relation to non-profit-seeking activities, is that Companies A and B have very widely dispersed shareholding, whereas in Company C there are large family shareholders, many of whom have long-standing family traditions of philanthropy and who, in agreeing to company benefactions for their own sake rather than for purely business reasons, are in a real sense giving their own money away.

Company foundations and trusts

Foundations, which are particular types of legal persons according to the country concerned, are nevertheless recognizably similar. They are non-profit, non-governmental organizations endowed with capital and managed by trustees which allocate the trusts' income to charitable, educational, cultural and other purposes accepted as beneficial to the community as a whole. Definitions of what constitutes a charity, limitations both as to geographical areas and spheres of activity, and tax deductibility are in some countries drawn rather narrower than in England and considerably narrower than in the United States. In the latter there has been a very rapid growth of foundations to the present total of over 30,000 (not all, of course, company sponsored or with funds directly from industrial fortunes). This figure of course includes foundations of all sizes, but at least twenty-six of them have assets of over $100 million, and foundations are now estimated to have $20 billion assets and make grants totalling $1.5 billion per year. In Britain there is only a very small number of foundations disposing of incomes of £500,000 or more. Although these larger trusts have almost all been founded upon personal fortunes derived from industry and often bear a company name, they may now be receiving income from other sources and are managed by trustees who are independent of any operating business company (e.g. the Nuffield Foundation). This is not necessarily true of some of the smaller company foundations endowed with company shares and with a preponderance of trustees drawn from the company board (or in the case of a family firm, from large family shareholders). The use of such company foundations as a vehicle for company philanthropy has both advantages and disadvantages. One of its advantages is that the company, having decided what sums it wishes to allocate to charitable purposes, can make the necessary transferrals and then hive off this activity to a separate body which is more appropriately organized for dispensing grants than a business company. Trustees can be appointed who are more expert and experienced in assessing the relative merits of applicants and, provided an income of at least £30,000–40,000 is generated, the trust can employ a competent administrator who can ensure that the use of grants is checked and evaluated. In making grants to research, pioneer social experiments and similar projects, the independence and impartiality of the trust must be without question. A close connection with a businesss company which might not be unaffected by the results of a research project might detract from the acceptability of its findings.

On the other hand, to achieve such separation and independence of a foundation from the company which has sponsored and endowed it means that the company can look for no business benefit direct or indirect of any kind from its philanthropy. This, apart from imposing a rather rigorous self-denying ordinance on company boards, raises the question again of why a public company spends money on objects which expressly exclude benefit to the company.

Also, as noted earlier, a company foundation properly staffed supposes a larger endowment than many companies may envisage in their charity budget. One way of dealing with this has been tried in America where consortia of small foundations have been formed with one salaried director (e.g. Kansas City Association of Trusts and Foundations).

Problems which can arise from the growth of company foundations have recently been reviewed in America and new rules have been legislated to prevent abuse of charitable status for other than philanthropic purposes. Some smaller company foundations had become suspect as being more concerned with tax avoidance or perpetuating control of family businesses than with supporting charities, and even the largest independent foundations have been under fire both in Congress and in public discussion for failing to give sufficient information about their activities and for maintaining too great a proportion of their funds in the shares of the business companies which created them. Charitable institutions as shareholders, it has been argued, may have conflicting interests with other shareholders in the matter of company gifts, and might in some circumstances be pressured to vote with management for fear of subsequently losing customary donations.[1]

Included in a wide-ranging tax reform enacted in December 1969[2] were new provisions governing the conduct and tax status of foundations and other exempt private organizations, as well as more limited tax deductibility for individual donors of charitable contributions. In future foundations will be subject to an annual audit tax of 4 per cent on net annual investment income, and they will have to distribute all net income or at least 6 per cent of their assets with a penalty tax of 15 per cent for failure to comply. The combined holdings of foundations and their officers is limited to 50 per cent of any single business and foundations with stock ownership in excess of this amount must divest themselves of it within fifteen years, while in future foundations must limit their holding of a corporation's voting stock to 20 per cent. Self dealing between foundations and their donors and operators is prohibited, and the use of foundation

---

[1] See 'Corporate Charitable Donations' (1969), 52 *Columbia Journal of Law & Social Problems*, 99.
[2] HR 13270.

funds in a way which might affect political campaigns is forbidden except for non-partisan efforts to improve voter registration.[1] More exacting regulations will now govern the disclosure of information regarding the activities of foundations and exempt private organizations and the taxation of their income derived from sources unrelated to charitable purposes. These and other changes are evidence of the way in which charitable giving by corporations if it reaches large proportions (and in 1967 gifts from company-sponsored foundations in USA were estimated at the dollar equivalent of £380 million)[2] will bring upon itself severe scrutiny as to its business connections, its political influence and its bona fide charitable activities.

Without a closer study of the functioning of existing company foundations in Britain it is difficult to weigh their advantages as a means of exercising corporate social obligations. A study has been undertaken for the European Cultural Foundation of certain aspects of foundations and charities in a number of European countries and, when completed, this will be of particular interest to companies who want to review the rationale of their corporate charity, especially if they want to consider extending their benefactions by setting up a company foundation.

In addition to the large and well-known foundations linked still by name if by no closer connection with industrial benefactors, there are substantial numbers of smaller company trusts and foundations. The history of one such company foundation indicates some of the advantages and disadvantages of these as a vehicle for company giving.

Company X Foundation is a company trust founded by a family-dominated 'close' company operating in one locality. Before 1945 the company was much smaller and did not think it was in a position to make charitable donations, but in subsequent years it grew rapidly and now has about £20 million assets and £3 million annual profits and is the principal employer in its locality. Stimulated by the special interest of the chairman, the board agreed in 1959 to allocate £70,000 per year in a seven-year covenant to provide finance for a company foundation.

From 1960 to 1964 the policy of the trustees was to spend sparingly and to build up capital in the fund. During this period, £83,000 was given and another £25,000 (spread over the next five years) promised. The trust deliberately restricted its benefactions to the locality in

---

[1] *Congressional Quarterly*, 9 January 1970.
[2] *Given in the USA*, The American Association of Fund raising Counsel, 1968.

which the company operates and, with the exception of a modest grant to a nearby university, supported recreational, social and cultural facilities in its own neighbourhood. From 1964 to 1967 the total of annual grants has ranged between £18,000 and £22,000 and the trust's objectives have been widened to include grants to schools, educational research and to a very limited number of social welfare projects. In this period, of the £58,500 allocated just under 50 per cent went to sports and recreational facilities and public amenities, a quarter on education (schools) and another fifth on higher education and research, and the balance on social welfare. The sums allocated as grants to state schools are noteworthy, these being an objective which some companies and foundations would not now consider suitable for aid because this involves a direct subsidy to relieve public funds. This kind of financing arises from the concern of the trust with immediate local educational needs as well as broader educational policies, and from the fact that some family and board members themselves play an active part in local educational administration.

Virtually all projects supported are related to the area in which the company and some of its employees (although it is not easy any longer for the company to be sure that it is serving the interests of its employees by subsidizing local causes because it now increasingly draws its workers from a much wider area) are located, and the policy of the trust is thus deliberately parochial both as a matter of business and because it is believed to be the best use to which funds can be put. The trust is even chary of spreading its gifts in the surrounding region because the trustees feel they can only know and properly judge the merits of strictly local appeals.

By 1964 the trustees had to reconsider their policy. The Inland Revenue queried their entitlement to a tax rebate on an expenditure of only £12,000 while the Foundation's resources stood at over £350,000. The trustees agreed that larger sums should be spent but felt that if an annual expenditure of some £30,000 was contemplated, a review of the foundation's policy and finances was essential with a view to clarifying objectives and appointing an administrator. In any case, with a change of chairman, the company's board was not willing automatically to renew covenants, since they were not prepared to contemplate the development over the next five years of a fund which could rise to £2–3 million, disposing of an income of perhaps £80,000 –100,000 per year, without a full review of the foundation's policy and administration.

From discussions it emerged that some members of the board felt that too much money had been spent in small amounts rather than concentrating grants upon a few larger and more significant contributions and that professional knowledge and administration should replace the *ad hoc* sponsorship of individual trustees. The division of opinion about the future of the foundation was broadly a generational one and was closely concerned with what pattern of family and company control ought to be maintained over the policies and activities of the foundation.

After a study of other company trusts and foundations carried out by one of the directors a report was made to the trustees with the following recommendations:

1 A competent administrator should be appointed by the trustees, *not* by the company (with secretarial assistance as necessary).
2 The foundation should settle the broad lines of policy, e.g. x per cent to be allocated to education.
3 Individual trustees should not have the power to override the administrator in promoting their special interests.
4 Outside experts should be appointed as a panel or on the management committee.
5 A local sub-committee should be appointed to make small local gifts (up to £50) within a budget of £1,000.
6 The trust should not become involved in the direct management of any project.

It was envisaged in the report that the administrator would sift all appeals and help to shape those that seemed worthy of consideration for presentation to the trustees; and that he would oversee the spending of grants and report upon their effectiveness. The report's description of the kind of man required clearly arose, from the need not merely to appoint a person competent to handle the business affairs of a trust disposing of £50,000–60,000 per year, but also for a personality able to deal with trustees who are family, board members, and important shareholders, and who are largely giving away their own money. In discussing the report, it was suggested by some board members that 'family cement' and 'local narrow interests' were an insufficient basis for a trust with the resources and potentialities envisaged. It was also noted that the present policy of doing good quietly in a local area and eschewing publicity and national appeals would not long survive the trust's emergence as a substantial grant-making body, and that a competent administrator and a well-articulated grant policy would be necessary to protect the trustees from importunate applicants. To appoint such an administrator while keeping administrative expense within 10 per cent supposes an income for the trust of at least £40,000. No decision on the future of the foundation has yet been reached.

This company's experience illustrates some of the difficulties of embarking upon a company trust as a way of meeting a company's philanthropic obligations. Without a clear decision about the relations of the company board and the company trust, and without a long-term development plan based on a definitive statement of the trust's objectives and geared to appropriate financial resources, a trust's funds may be unduly hoarded or frittered away without significant results. If this happens there is no particular advantage in a company trust over a policy of *ad hoc* covenanted donations to individual charities. Money may still be doled out according to the interests and influence of board members or the relative pressure and nuisance value of applicants. There may, of course, be good business reasons for a company wishing to control its gifts through a company trust, but this is another kind of consideration which ought to be made explicit.

It must also be said that the desire of some board members and trustees for a clear policy and a competent administrator (and by implication fewer grants settled by enthusiastic individual sponsorship) sounds businesslike but may be a little unrealistic. Where voluntary efforts are needed for new social projects, and independent funds have to be raised for minority interests, the enthusiasm and persistence of individual sponsors is often essential. Similarly, a demand for the complete independence of trustees from any company influence is unlikely to be achieved, at any rate in the early stages of development, in a foundation which has been wholly sponsored and financed by a family firm.

Amounts given by companies of varying sizes

The amount given by industry over the last ten years (1958–67) as a percentage of company profits has risen steadily (apart from a slight fall back in 1964 and 1965) from 0.28 per cent in 1958 to 0.42 per cent in 1967, i.e. by 50 per cent.

Tables II, III, and IV show how these total sums allocated by companies to charitable objects are distributed by net income and by size of payments.

Tables I and II show the sums specified as transfers of company income to charities in the *National Income and Expenditure* accounts, and though not including all, probably include much the greater part of all company donations in the United Kingdom.[1] The Companies

---

[1] A major part of the donations of international companies is often distributed by their divisions or subsidiaries overseas. Companies in Britain also make gifts in kind and indefinite loans of equipment.

TABLE I: *Company Donations to Charities as a Percentage of Gross Company Profits and Net Company Income 1958–67*

Year	1958	1959	1960	1961	1962	1963	1964	1965	1966	1967
Company transfers to charity, £ million	13	15	17	19	21	24	26	28	30	32
% of gross company profits	0.28	0.30	0.31	0.35	0.38	0.39	0.37	0.37	0.41	0.42
% of net company income	0.35	0.37	0.39	0.45	0.51	0.54	0.53	0.52	0.55	0.54

Source: National Income and Expenditure 1968, HMSO, Table 30.

* Gross company profits less capital allowances as shown in *National Income and Expenditure 1968*, p. 105.

TABLE II: *Company Contributions to Charities 1964*

£ million

	(a) Covenanted payments	(b) Subscriptions and donations (disallowed)	Total (a) and (b)
Payments by individuals	5	No information	No information
Payments by companies with more than £100,000 net true income*	4½	1½	6
Payments by companies with less than £100,000 net true income	15½	4½	20
Total company payments	20	6	26
Total payments	25	No information	No information

Source: From a sample enquiry made by Inland Revenue, 1964.

* Net true income is gross income less allowances for repairs to land and buildings and capital allowances.

TABLE III: *Number of Companies' Donations to Charities by Size of Payments, 1964*

Range of payments to charities £	Number of companies	
	Covenants	Donations and subscriptions
Nil	205	75
0–100	39	126
100–1,000	89	177
1,000–10,000	79	54
10,000 and over	30	10
Total	442	442

Source: From a sample enquiry by Inland Revenue, 1964.

Act 1967 now requires companies to publish the sum of their donations to charities but as this section of the Act applies only to company 'years' ending after January 1968, it will be some time before it is possible to see the full extent of company giving and whether publication of industrial donations is accompanied by any marked change in their scale.

In 1964, £26 million was donated (i.e. other than sums allowed as business expenses) by way of both covenanted payments (£20 million) and subscriptions and donations (£6 million). In that year a 10 per cent sample of companies showed (Table I) that although big companies may make the largest donations, in the aggregate the donations of the much larger number of smaller companies (less than £100,000 true net income) accounted for 77 per cent of the total given.

Companies within a range of net income of over £10 million gave larger absolute amounts on average than companies in smaller income groups. However, as a proportion of gross profits the very largest and the smallest companies gave at about the same rate, while the medium and medium-to-large sized companies gave at twice this rate. (Table IV.)

Forty-six per cent of companies made no covenanted payments and about 17 per cent gave no uncovenanted donations or subscriptions. A further 9 per cent gave less than £100 in covenants and 28 per cent less than £100 in donations. On the other hand, nearly 7 per cent covenanted to give over £10,000. (See Table IV.)

By 1967 the total sum transferred to charities in company accounts had risen to £32 million but no further information was available about the distribution of this amount until companies began to report their donations under the Companies Act 1967. In order to obtain a more recent picture of industrial donations, the accounts were examined of a random group of 10 per cent of companies with £500,000 net assets or profits over £50,000, reporting in the first months of 1968 on trading years which had ended in January or later of that year. Their reports have been analysed to see whether there appeared to be any significant relationships between company donations and any other major features of their financial or trading position.

Table V shows donations of a sample 10 per cent of companies with £500,000 capital employed or £50,000 net income or both, and within this category all sizes of companies and all industrial groupings, the distributive trades and service industries were represented.

TABLE IV: *Company Donations to Charities, 1964*

(Companies with over £100,000 net true income *only*, 10 per cent sample)

| Range of net true income £m | Sample results | | | (4) Gross profits £000 | Grossed results | | | (8) Col. 7 as % of Col. 4 | (9) Average Payments £ |
| | (1) Number | (2) Sampling fraction | (3) Number | | PAYMENTS TO CHARITIES £000 | | | | |
					(5) (a) Covenants	(6) (b) Donations	(7) (c) Total		
£0.01–0.2	92	5%	2,175	359,341	166	265	431	.12	200
£0.2–1.0	178	10%	1,931	970,815	1,943	661	2,604	.26	1,350
£1.0–2.0	66	30%	208	377,159	772	163	935	.25	4,500
£2.0–10.0	86	60%	141	568,463	1,096	325	1,421	.25	10,000
£10.0 and over	20	100%	20	477,591	460	155	615	.13	30,000
Total	442		4,314	2,753,369	4,437	1,569	6,006	.21	1,391
No information	24								
Grand Total	466								

Source: From a sample enquiry made by Inland Revenue, 1964.

TABLE V: *Random 10 per cent Group of Companies among the first Reporting Company Donations in 1968, by Capital Employed*

Capital employed £m	All companies* with net assets of £500,000 or profits over £50,000	Percentage in sample	No. in sample	Breakdown of sample %
5–1	507	5	25	11
1–2	487	10	48	21
2–4	383	10	40	17
4–8	274	11	31	14
8–16	182	10	19	8
16–32	183	9	17	7
32–64	72	22	18	8
64–128	38	30	11	5
128–256	26	57	13	6
256+	15	40	6	3
—	2,167		228	100

* Board of Trade, 1965.

TABLE VI: *Sample Companies by Numbers of Employees and Net Income*

Nos. of employees	Nos. of Companies	%	Range of net income £m	Nos. of Companies	%
100–300	17	7	0.5–0.75	131	57
300–500	26	11	0.75–1	14	6
500–1,000	42	18	1–3	27	12
1,000–3,000	58	26	3–7	23	10
3,000–10,000	38	17	7–10	6	3
10,000–25,000	26	11	10–15	10	4
25,000–50,000	13	6	15–20	6	3
50,000 and over	6	3	20 and over	7	3
Not available	2	1	Not available	4	2
Total	228	100	Total	228	100

These 228 companies (which did not include banks, insurance and investment companies, etc.) gave between them £2,157,691 to charities. The 30 per cent which made political donations gave in total £156,337. Forty-three per cent of companies gave more than £1,000

(cf. Table IV). Twenty-four companies (11 per cent) gave no donations at all, but no company gave political donations which did not
also give to charities.[1]

TABLE VII: *Amounts Given to Charities by 228 Companies*

Amount	No. of Companies	Per cent
Up to £100	21	8
£100–£500	61	27
£500–£1,000	24	11
£1,000–£5,000	46	20
£5,000–£20,000	20	9
£20,000–£50,000	20	9
£50,000+	12	5
No donations	24	11
Total	228	100

Donations: company size
These sums represent a very tiny fraction of capital employed (which
is a rough indicator of size and for which the figures are readily available). One hundred and ninety-five companies (84 per cent) gave less
than 0.1 per cent of capital employed. Nine companies (4 per cent)
gave between 0.1 and 0.5 per cent, and 24 (11 per cent) companies
made no donations at all.

Large companies gave the most in absolute terms, but if companies
in the sample are grouped by capital employed, donations in proportion to this capital employed follow a humped curve, the very largest
and the very smallest companies giving least, and the companies with
capital between £64 million and £128 million giving most (and this
pattern is confirmed by the official figures—see Table IV on page
111). However, if the companies which gave nothing are excluded, and
they were, with two exceptions, all smaller companies, one-fifth of the
group of companies with less than £1 million capital employed gave
more than 0.1 per cent of capital employed, compared with only five

[1] Since these figures were published many more donations including political
ones have been declared. 'Political donations amounted to £176,124 for those
companies which have sent a directors' report to the Board of Trade for financial
years ending on or after 26 January 1968, with net assets over £500,000 or profits
over £50,000.' *Hansard* Col. 315, 12 February 1969. By the same date, however,
the Labour Party had already noted political donations by companies totalling
£400,000. Thus political donations do not appear to have been reduced as a
result of the need to disclose them and indeed are reported to be already substantially higher than in former years.

113

companies out of the remaining 203. For the largest companies (those with more than £128 million capital), which gave between them £1.25 million, their donations only represented 0.03 per cent of capital employed and about 0.27 per cent of net income.

Donations: profits

TABLE VIII: *Company Donations as a Percentage of Net Company Incomes (228 companies)*

£ given per £1,000 of net income	No. of companies	Percentage of companies
Nil	24	11
Under £1	66	29
£1–£3	91	40
£3–£10	36	15
Over £10	11	5
Total	228	100

From Table VIII it can be seen that even as a percentage of their net income companies' donations are very small. The companies with the highest net incomes did not give proportionately the largest amounts. Of the eleven companies which gave more than 1 per cent, six were companies with less than £1 million net income, while no company with over £20 million net income gave at this rate. Of the twenty-three companies with the highest net incomes (£10 million and over) six gave between £3 and £7 per £1,000, sixteen gave less than £3 per £1,000, and only one gave £10 per £1,000 of net income.

Donations: directors' shareholdings

It is sometimes suggested that companies with concentrated directors' shareholdings are able to pursue non-profit-seeking activities more readily since they are less likely to encounter opposition from shareholders. The proportion of directors' shareholding, including their holdings as trustees, was examined in this group of 228 companies to see whether there was any correlation between these and the amounts given to charities, but our test did not show any relationship. The seventy-four companies (32 per cent) where directors' holdings either directly or as trustees were 20 per cent or more formed 39 per cent of the companies giving more than £10 per £1,000 of net income. On the other hand, among the companies where directors' shareholdings were less than 2 per cent (26 per cent of all companies), these formed 33 per cent of the companies making the largest donations as a proportion of net income.

Donations from the clearing banks and the Bank of England are not included in any amounts estimated here. Banks are reputed to give generously but usually prefer to be approached before appeals become public. The clearing banks have a joint committee which meets regularly to discuss support for charitable causes and there is a good deal of consultation generally in the City about appeals.

Objects for which companies make donations; local and national appeals
Funds donated are distributed to a variety of organizations recognized in law as charities. These range from local youth clubs to large national funds, and include education and research, the arts and public amenities as well as organizations for social welfare—more commonly thought of as charities.

An enquiry in 1957,[1] which reported on the donations of 232 companies in sixteen major industrial groups, found that in seven industries research, and in a further three education, took the largest share of money given. Together, education and research claimed well over half the sums donated in each industrial group except for commerce, clothing and footwear, consumer durables and service industries, and in these groups the largest amount of their donations went to social services.

A comparison with an analysis of company donations made three years later,[2] showed this trend continuing; 77 per cent of companies studied (sixty-two in total) gave to company related education and research and virtually all (97 per cent) gave to education and research of one kind or another.

TABLE IX: *Objects Supported by Donations among Sixty-two Companies*

Object	Supported per cent	Expressly excluded per cent
Education and research	97	
Company-related education and research	77	
General social welfare	97	
Company-related welfare	75	
Arts	44	16
Recreation and public amenities	75	
Religious causes		46

[1] *Business and the Community*, The Economist Intelligence Unit, 1957.
[2] An analysis based on material collected in an enquiry by the Federation of British Industries, 1960–2.

It must be noted that although company boards lay down general principles which instruct their managers and, where there is one, their Appeals Committee, these are not always strictly followed. Among twenty-eight companies (the 46 per cent of companies in Table IX) which stated that they did not think it appropriate to contribute to denominational religious causes, a third had in fact made such donations in the last year, and a further fifth had subscribed to the funds of cathedrals and national churches which perhaps were regarded as subscriptions for the preservation of historic buildings. On the other hand, eight out of the ten companies (16 per cent) who did not think that artistic endeavours should be eligible for company donations did in fact firmly exclude the arts from their benefactions.

It is clear both from Table IX and from the statements of company boards that one acceptable way of determining the destination if not the dimensions of corporate charity is to settle for grants to education and research. It is on the whole easier to justify educational expenditure as likely to yield a direct if unquantifiable benefit to companies as well as serving the public interest. It is less likely to provoke an adverse reaction from the shareholders than patronizing the arts or giving to denominational religious causes. Shell, for example, does not give to the latter but the company has a direct interest in the supply of scientists and in research and has therefore contributed to higher education at the rate of well over £100,000 per year. Between 1953 and 1962, every university and college of science and technology in the UK received some financial assistance from Shell which, 'excluding research (as distinct from education) represented an outlay of over £1,000,000'.[1]

Unilever and ICI similarly allocate about half of all their donations to higher education and research and the majority of companies studied irrespective of size gave over half (in £ value) of their donations to education in some form.

The pattern of company giving shown in Table X relates only to sixty-two[2] companies for which detailed information was available and this group included very few small companies. Two-thirds of these companies had over £25 million capital employed and 95 per cent had over 2,000 employees. Among these larger companies, donations were substantial:

20 companies gave up to £5,000
15 companies gave between £5,000 and £20,000
17 companies gave between £20,000 and £70,000
10 companies gave £70,000 or more

[1] *Shell Grants* 1963.
[2] Federation of British Industries, *op. cit.*

TABLE X: *Objects of Company Donations by Amounts Given*
(Sixty-two Companies)

Objects	Per cent	£
1. Education: company-related	26 ⎫62	498,820
other	36 ⎭	689,259
2. Social welfare: company-related	2 ⎫20	37,625
other	18 ⎭	340,826
3. Arts: company-related	1 ⎫1	794
other	⎭	19,209
4. Religious bodies	4.4	84,067
5. Health services (hospitals etc.) and medical research	6.4	122,445
6. Miscellaneous (including public amenities, recreation, historic buildings and Service charities not included under (2))	6.2	118,946
Total	100.0	£1,912,092

Among the ten largest, three gave over £200,000 (not all dispensed in Britain), two gave between £100,000 and £150,000, and five between £70,000 and £100,000. Between them these sixty-two companies gave directly[1] nearly £2 million. All but 2 per cent gave single donations and subscriptions and 80 per cent also gave by way of covenants. Half of the companies not entering into covenants had their own company trusts.

From Table X it can be seen that the value of donations which could be said to be identifiably connected with the company's business and employees amounted to 28 per cent of the total, and was mostly accounted for by gifts to higher education and research.

Half the companies gave something to the arts but the amounts were limited. Only one company gave over £5,000 and two others over £2,500 and two over £1,000 respectively. The rest of the companies' gifts were of much smaller sums; a third of them were less than £100. Individual companies of course have given handsomely to

[1] Some companies (fourteen) had their own charitable trusts or foundations and sums transferred to these are additional to their other direct gifts. International companies give also through their overseas companies. This figure (£2 million) therefore understates the total amount of donations in this group of companies.

the arts but most companies seem hesitant to divert much of the shareholders' money to artistic endeavours.[1] These sums do not include any patronage of the arts by companies which furnish their boardrooms or executive suites with *objets d'art*, or who purchase the services of artists for industrial design or advertising. This kind of expenditure is treated as allowable business expenses, not as company donations.

Although the largest *number* of donations were given locally, because companies feel they should respond to appeals from the local community in which they do business, the *value* of local gifts was only 18 per cent of all donations, whereas 64 per cent of moneys donated were given to national funds or to the national headquarters of organizations. The balance of donations, another 18 per cent, was accounted for by overseas appeals. It must be remembered that this is an allocation of funds between local and national appeals among a group of predominantly large companies. If more smaller companies were included local gifts might represent a larger part of total funds.

Company attitudes to charitable giving

In addition to the sixty-two companies for whom details of their donations were available, another twenty-four companies, making eighty-six in total, gave information about the way they arrived at their decisions. About one-third (34 per cent) had a formal Appeals Committee, and only 6 per cent said they consulted with other companies, though this may have omitted some very informal discussions between company chairmen. In deciding the amount to be given, 19 per cent said it was a matter of prestige and good public relations and that a large well-known company might provoke unfavourable comment if it gave nothing or substantially less than its peers. Twelve per cent of companies said the size of their donations depended on the state of trade and 39 per cent that it depended on the state of the donations budget.

General attitudes to company philanthropy are hard to disentangle, and in classifying companies broadly below the writer has had to exercise some discretion in trying to 'record and report what she thinks they will think that they ought to have thought'! With this qualification Table XI shows the proportions of the eighty-six companies which volunteered that these considerations listed had the greatest influence on their policies.

[1] For a thoughtful study of industrial support for the arts in Britain see Trevor Russell Cobb, *Paying the Piper*, Queen Anne Press, 1968. Also R. Eells, *The Corporation and the Arts*, Arkville Press, USA, 1967.

TABLE XI: *Company Attitudes to Charitable Donations* (*eighty-six companies: multiple statements*)

Per cent

A *Company donations are mainly undertaken:*

1. For good business reasons, related to long-term business needs, etc. — 38

2. To accommodate customers, other business colleagues on a 'knock-for knock' basis, etc. — 21

3. As an obligation *faute de mieux* in the absence of large private donors and patrons — 35

4. Because of the special interest of the chairman or managing director — 21

5. Because the board positively approved of this as a business responsibility and are actively interested — 29

— 64
(Favoured giving)

6. Because they are accepted indifferently as usual business practice — 21

— 21
(Indifferent)

B *Charitable appeals to companies are criticized as:*

1. Taking too much time — 7

2. Exerting too much pressure on top executives — 13

3. Being undertaken cynically for purely self-interested motives — 3

— 23
(Critical)

Companies gave more than one reason, of course, for their donations and broadly they can be grouped into:

Per cent

1 Those who positively and actively believed in company giving — 29

2 Those who accepted it as a company duty — 35

3 Those who were critical or cynical — 15

4 Those who were largely indifferent — 21

100

This group of companies, though including most industrial classifications and areas of the country, included very few smaller companies (less than fifty employees and/or less than £100,000 capital employed) and therefore did not represent their views.

The great majority of companies, even those which complained about requests for donations, went to a great deal of trouble in sifting appeals. Most often these were dealt with at board level and a good deal of highly-paid time was sometimes expended deciding on a £50 donation to a local boys' club. Some companies had delegated preliminary sifting to junior staff but this could be unsatisfactory unless they were experienced. An inexperienced person might throw out an appeal on the grounds that the charity had too high administrative costs without observing that the charity was perhaps a counselling agency in which the salaries of professional staff legitimately formed a very substantial part of expenses. One junior assistant said he threw out all the 'glossy' appeals because if the charity spent money on expensive printing it probably was not really short of funds, but he put forward all the handwritten letters because he thought they came from more genuine causes. Where there were appeals committees and explicit donations policies there was still a good deal of flexibility about the way they were operated.

American business philanthropy
Corporate philanthropy is widely accepted in the United States as a company duty and the estimated total for charitable giving in the United States in 1967 amounted to the dollar equivalent of £6,070 million, of which business contributions were £380 million.[1] Company-sponsored foundations, the numbers of which are rapidly increasing, gave as much again.

Company contributions amount to around 1 per cent of net company income (1.14 per cent in 1967) before tax and provide about 12.5 per cent of all philanthropic giving.[2]

The distribution of company donations by American companies in 1967 was to:

Health and welfare	40 per cent
Education	40 per cent
Civic and cultural objects	20 per cent

Formerly about 75 per cent of the company donations went to health and welfare, but now education shares equally.[3] Even so, business contributes only 2 per cent of the cost of higher education. An enquiry by the Nation Industrial Conference Board (1966–8)

[1] *Giving in the USA*, The American Association of Fund raising Counsel, 1968.
[2] *Statistics of Income*, US Treasury Department, 1966.
[3] See also K. G. Patrick and R. Eells, *Education and the Business Dollar*, Arkville Press, 1967.

among a thousand companies with more than 500 employed found that 92 per cent made some donations. A rather greater proportion of the large companies (94 per cent) did so than among the smaller companies (88 per cent).

Two practices widespread in the United States influence the pattern of American giving. 'Community' drives in each locality for 'community chests' and united funds reduce the multiplicity and duplication of fund-raising campaigns and keep down their cost. Every group in the community is expected to take part, and 1–2 per cent of their net profit is expected from companies. Some firms also allow their staff to assist in campaigns, and facilitate the collection of contributions from their employees. From the companies' point of view the number of conflicting demands is reduced, they are relieved of making invidious choices between charities (the community-chest organization allocates funds raised) and the distractions of fund-raising are concentrated in one period of time.

The second feature is the widespread use of professional fund-raisers. The use of fund-raisers, long established in America, has grown very rapidly there[1] and has produced a new professional service in which experienced staff apply sophisticated techniques to the organization of charitable appeals. There are, of course, well-established reputable fund-raising consultants in Britain, but it is only more recently that they have come to play a major role in the organization of charitable appeals. Since, to make the cost of professional help worth while, substantial sums have to be raised, professional appeals' organizers often try first to secure promises of significant company donations. Their experience is that a businesslike presentation of an appeal with relevant information and clear financial objectives more readily commends itself to most company boards than the unorganized enthusiasm of volunteers. In the course of careful market research before launching appeals, professional fund-raisers learn what kind of cause is likely to be welcomed by which companies and they are less likely to confuse and irritate businessmen than some of the blunderbuss fund-raising efforts of charities themselves. Some companies consulted complained of letters from charities addressed to long deceased chairmen, etc.

'People launching appeals often seem not to inform themselves on the most elementary points . . . Organizations having secured a large subscription or covenant from a company make no effort thereafter to provide an annual report or accounts' (company secretary).

[1] See also 'The American Way of Giving', *The Economist*, 26 December 1964, p. 1422.

THE SIGNIFICANCE OF COMPANY DONATIONS FOR CHARITABLE FUND-RAISING

Though the sums given to charities are not of great significance in the total finances of most British companies, being generally less than half of one per cent of net income and very much less as a percentage of capital employed, industrial donations are of the greatest importance to the charities themselves. General charities dependent upon public donations turn to companies in the hope of larger gifts than private donors are likely to make. Educational bodies look to industry to supplement the inadequacies of public finance and the modest contributions of alumni, especially for new capital developments and for research funds. Every new university and most of the older ones have launched public appeals to supplement the funds of the official University Grants Committee, mainly for capital developments like new halls of residence. In twelve such appeals launched by red-brick universities, in 1959–64, industrial contributions supplied in no case less than 40 per cent and in some cases as much as 90 per cent of the funds raised.

Similarly, the new universities have found that apart from the local authorities and trusts, the bulk of their special appeals fund is donated by companies. Industrial giving for education is concentrated mainly on higher education; independent schools obtain only a small proportion of their funds from industry (boys' schools 9 per cent, and girls' schools 4 per cent).[1] The 'popular' charities which evoke ready response, e.g. those dealing with children and old people's welfare, are supported by industry but expect to raise the bulk of their funds from the general public.

In medical research, finance from governmental sources and research expenditures by the pharmaceutical industry have both increased threefold within a decade but contributions to medical charities (including research) have risen even faster and draw substantial industrial support. In addition to spending about £9 million (one-third of all expenditure on medical research) as part of its business, the pharmaceutical industry donated a further £280,000 (in 1961) for research from which no direct benefit to the companies concerned was expected. About 14 per cent of the expenditure of £27 million (1961–2) on medical research came from medical research charities,[2] e.g. the British Empire Cancer Campaign, the Arthritis and Rheumatism Research Council, the Mental Health Research Fund,

[1] Public Schools Commission. The percentages are 13 for boys and 5 for girls if contributions from the Industrial Fund are added; see p. 124 below.
[2] *The Finance of Medical Research*, Office of Health Economics, 1964.

etc., and trusts in which industrial contributions play a notable part. The Wellcome Trust is unique in the United Kingdom[1] among charitable bodies assisting research in that its income is derived from a pharmaceutical firm (the Wellcome Foundation Ltd.) in which the Trustees hold all the share capital. Between 1964 and 1966, £2,500,000 was given in grants to medical research bringing the total grants from this Foundation to £9,500,000 since its inception (1936).

On the other hand, charities which have little popular appeal either because they are controversial or cater for very specialized interests do not easily commend themselves to industrial donors. A body like the National Council for the Unmarried Mother and her Child, whose work is seriously hampered for lack of funds, received (in 1967) less than £1,000 from companies, about 15 per cent of its annual income. Thirty-six companies, including some of the largest, made contributions but these tended to be token contributions of £25 to £50.

Ought companies to be encouraged to allocate more company funds to donations? Those who think they should often recommend a change in tax incentives, such as permitting a fixed percentage of company income or turnover to be tax deductible for charitable purposes. They point out that the tax treatment of charitable gifts in Britain is unusual in that the donor (including companies), as distinct from the recipient, receives no special fiscal dispensation. This is in contrast to the practice in America and some continental European countries where company gifts are deductible up to 5 per cent (and, in some special cases, 10 per cent), of taxable income. It is sometimes argued that permitting a fixed percentage for tax deductibility would encourage British companies to give at least as generously as American ones, i.e. 1 per cent of company income, which would be twice the amount now given. On the other hand it would be difficult to press for the introduction of a fixed limit for tax deductibility as in America and still expect to keep also the procedure for gifts by covenant. The time is probably overdue for a review of the tax treatment of donors both corporate and private, but the advantages of the covenant system especially to the charities should not be overlooked in any proposals for change.

It has been suggested that company contributions could be collected with less trouble and focused more effectively on socially useful projects, if businessmen combined their efforts. One example of joint action by a number of companies was the Industrial Fund for the Advancement of Scientific Education in Schools. This trust was

[1] The Carlsberg Breweries in Copenhagen have for fifty years devoted their entire distributable profits to the promotion of science and the arts through the Carlsberg Foundation.

set up in 1955 with the object of increasing the output of scientists and technologists by giving assistance to schools in building, expanding and equipping school laboratories. This was a fund which raised £3.2 million exclusively (with one exception) from company donations under a committee of prominent businessmen. Grants were purposely only made to independent schools because they were unable to get grants of public money, and to some 'direct grant' schools. The Fund appointed highly qualified and experienced assessors who visited the schools and, within the general policy laid down by the committee, made recommendations for appropriate payments. By arranging an overdraft (at a cost of no more than 3.5 per cent of total expenditure) capital developments were able to be started before all the subscriptions were gathered in, and £2.6 million was allocated for building grants and £387,000 for apparatus. With the help of two large companies subscribing to the fund, administrative costs were kept to one-eighth of 1 per cent. Assistance which varied from new science blocks to minor improvements, was limited to two-thirds of approved costs. After the original enquiry, the schools were twice surveyed again (in 1959 and 1962) and a detailed follow-up and assessment made for the Fund by its chief assessor. Evaluation of the effectiveness of the use of grants could only be tentative because of the difficulty of distinguishing between the grants and other coincidental developments. With this qualification, the numbers specializing in science and mathematics at Advanced Level had increased by about 40 per cent, the arts sections of sixth-forms were experimenting with science courses, and it had become a general rule in the schools helped that every boy would study a science subject up to 'O' level. Some of the schools helped by the Fund had doubled their numbers in their science and mathematics sixth-forms.

There were two other beneficial fall-outs from the Fund's activities. In assessing schools' needs, standards for space and equipment were evolved and an architectural brochure devised for the special needs of school laboratories. The latter was reprinted and has been widely used outside the schools concerned with the Fund. This and other aspects of the Fund's work received widespread interest in other countries and a scheme based upon the UK Fund was developed in Australia.

This Fund is an example of the kind of giving which may be appropriate for joint action by industrial companies, and which is innovative, that is going out to meet a need, rather than merely responding to appeals.

The object, better science teaching facilities, could not be achieved by calling on public funds, and yet served both business and the public interest. The aim of the fund was quite specific and did not involve businessmen in a confusion of choice between equally worthy causes, or in themselves making invidious choices between different schools. The assessment of need was made by professional advisers on the basis of explicit criteria, and, in the process, standards of space and design of general value were evolved. The Fund was managed as a business investment employing skilled help, keeping down administrative costs, and by using loans it commenced and completed capital developments promptly. This was a project in which 141 companies surrendered willingly their sovereignty as donors, which suggests that the objection that companies would never agree to some industrial contributions being channelled through one central fund may not be as strong as is sometimes supposed.

A central fund for industrial donations

One proposal[1] which from time to time is made for handling charitable appeals to industry is that companies could pay a levy (perhaps based on a formula such as a percentage of net income, turnover or payroll), into a central fund from which allocations would be made to recognized charities. The grounds on which this is advocated are usually:

(a) To reduce the nuisance to companies of dealing with a multiplicity of appeals.

(b) To apply professional attention and knowledge to the selection of appeals worth supporting; this could include:

    (i) a thorough pre-scrutiny to determine an appeal's relevance to British industry and what proportion of the appeal target industry might reasonably be expected to find, and

    (ii) a follow up and post-audit on the effectiveness of grants made.

(c) To ease the pressure on the large and better-known companies which are the immediate target for all fund-raisers, and to see that charitable donations are stimulated[2] among companies not at present contributing.

(d) To give a guide to appropriate charity budgets especially for smaller companies which may be deterred from putting in their mites by the size of donations made by larger companies.

---

[1] This idea was carefully explored by Sir Eric Coates for the Federation of British Industries (1960–2), but there did not seem to be sufficient support at that time for the idea to be pursued further.

[2] Tables III and IV on pages 109 and 111 above suggested that contributions are more widespread among small companies than is often realized.

(e) To avoid the reciprocal pressure on the 'old boy' network which sometimes occurs now and which cannot be said to encourage discriminating benevolence.

The objections to a central fund are, among others, that:

(1) Giving would become impersonal, companies would lose interest and would be even less concerned than they are now with the charities their gifts help to support.

(2) Companies want to have their names associated with their gifts and this is an entirely proper way in which boards derive some benefit (i.e. good public relations) for their company.

(3) Companies must retain full responsibility for the purpose(s), including donations, to which the shareholders' money is put.

(4) No time or trouble would be saved because companies would still be approached by individual charities which had been unsuccessful with the Central Fund, and where local interests were involved the company might find itself making a second donation and in effect giving twice.

(5) A central fund which is operated as an *administrative* organ for receiving and carrying out company instructions is unnecessary as a perfectly good one exists already in the Charities Aid Fund. A central fund which is operated as an *advisory bureau* might have some value, but again the Charities Aid Fund performs this service already and if it were deemed necessary its present advisory service could be extended. A central fund which is operated as an *executive* body with power to grant aid would inevitably develop fairly uniform policies, encouraging some types of appeal and firmly excluding others. This would destroy one of the main justifications for industrial gifts, namely that they represent a variety of decisions dispersed through the community about which charities, which arts, or which research ought to be encouraged.

These advantages and objections may be stronger in relation to certain types of donations than to others. For example, it is difficult to see how local causes supported because of local commercial interest could be brought within the framework of a central fund. On the other hand, *ad hoc* national appeals which usually bring no direct business benefit to individual companies (except to have their name in small print on a long subscription list no one reads), might well be an area in which industry as a whole could agree to a *pro rata* levy from companies without the time, trouble and expense involved now in approaching individual firms. It may be, moreover, that many of the advantages of a single central fund without the drawbacks could be obtained from a number of groups of firms, whether organized locally or regionally (like the American community chests), or by industry, or on some other basis.

REVIEW OF THE RATIONALE AND FUTURE DEVELOPMENT OF COMPANY GIVING

Why should business companies make donations to charities at all? Except where such donations can be justified on business grounds, they would appear to be prima facie outside the companies' proper sphere of activity and an unwarrantable use of their funds. If, despite the prima facie appearance of the matter, they are justified, this must depend upon special reasons not rooted in the companies' business purposes; and the champions of company giving other than for business purposes must produce such reasons and show that they can survive scrutiny.

If company giving is justified, whether on business or on other grounds, the question then arises whether its organization is efficient. Are companies' methods of giving well devised? Do they achieve their aims? are there ways in which company giving ought to be developed and expanded? These questions also need to be considered but first it must be shown that making company donations is justifiable.

It is clear that much company giving is justified on sound business grounds. Obliging particular customers; creating goodwill in an area of company operation or in its catchment area for the recruitment of labour; increasing the supply of educated or technically qualified persons for the purpose of future recruitment; supporting business-related research (e.g. tobacco companies and cancer research); improving the company's public image generally; perhaps also seeking to impress those who look with a jaundiced eye on large profits by devoting a part of them to good causes: these are among the reasons for giving which are consistent with business purposes.

What presents difficulty in practice in relation to company giving for business reasons is, first, the fact that the return cannot be quantified, and, secondly, the fact that in many cases business reasons are mixed with non-business reasons. In such cases justification must be sought on non-business grounds, for the justification of expenditure to serve business ends depends not only on the character of those ends but also on the adequacy of the business return.

127

The essential arguments for company giving on non-business grounds are twofold:

1. The modern corporation must take the place of the former private patron *faute de mieux*. It is an obligation which may be unsought but cannot be escaped. The activities of independent charitable institutions would be greatly reduced without gifts from business, and if it is desired that such institutions should survive business must provide some of their funds. Apart from the State and some trusts founded formerly from private fortunes, only business is now likely to be able to dispose of the large resources needed to enable charities to fulfil their purposes.

2. Business would have a positive social responsibility to support charity, even if there were a satisfactory supply of private patronage. Companies are the stewards of large amounts of the community's resources, and some part of their wealth (accumulated with the aid of the privilege of limited liability) should be returned to the community. Giving is as much a moral duty of the company as it is of the private citizen, and since companies have much greater resources than individuals, it is they who should be the example for others.

Clearly there is much that is debatable in these arguments. The contention that only companies dispose of sufficient funds independently of the State must obviously be qualified in view of the fact that a substantial part of the donations charities receive from them are really the State's contribution in tax forgone. Furthermore the same funds would be available for charitable giving if they were distributed to shareholders (in the United Kingdom). Since corporation tax and the standard rate of income tax are now almost the same, the fact that covenanted payments are not allowed against surtax does not in theory leave giving by shareholders at a disadvantage compared with giving by companies, i.e. the quantum of tax saving is the same and the difference between company and shareholder giving is therefore a difference in the locus of decision making not in the availability of funds from which gifts could be made. It may however be true that in practice sur-taxable individuals are less likely to make charitable covenants than companies free of tax other than corporation tax.

Secondly, what is the basis of a company board's legal right to allocate assets for non-business purposes? Is it simply that the shareholders do not object (which in practice appears to be universally the case)? This may be said to settle the matter. On the other hand it may be objected that this is a result of shareholder ignorance and inattention of just the kind which some company law reformers see as the product of board powers which ought to be amended. Furthermore, suppose that a minority of shareholders do object. In equity ought the majority to have the right to impose a non-business use of their assets on the minority?

Alternatively, the board's right is based upon the proposition that the company's assets are not properly to be regarded as shareholders' assets. On this view the facts that the shareholders (or their predecessors) put up the company's original equity, and that the shareholders have the right to appoint and dismiss their board, do not justify the contention that the company's funds are shareholders' funds. The funds belong to the company until they are distributed, and the board is trustee for the company as a separate entity from the shareholders. Hence, until it is dismissed the board may dispose of the company's assets in any way which is not *ultra vires* the Memorandum and Articles of Association and which is not done in bad faith from the point of view of trusteeship for the company.

Thirdly, what special competence have company boards to decide which private institutions for, say, education, the arts, or social welfare merit financial assistance? If they have none, can it be right for them to use their powers to apply company funds to these purposes? In answer it may be said that it is not necessary for boards to have such a special competence. First, they can appoint those who have it to act for them, by establishing independent foundations, for example, or taking the advice of an expert intermediary like the Charities Aid Fund. Secondly, since there is no uniquely right policy in charitable giving, there is merit in any system which disperses initiative among givers. Hence, to spread these decisions among all sizes of companies and among businessmen of differing views is in itself desirable. But it implies that special expertness in the process of giving cannot be a condition of its justification.

Fourthly, objection may be made to the power of patronage embodied in company giving. It may be said that institutions like, say, universities which come to depend heavily on business donations may find that they have added to the State another over-powerful master—big business. Will the increase of company donations to universities and research institutes come to shape their work towards industry's needs—more of applied science, technology and business studies and less of arts and humanities? Against this two things may be said. First, the prevailing characteristic of business in its donations policy appears to be caution and sensitiveness to public opinion. Secondly, to the extent that company giving seeks to bend academic work to serve business interests, then such charitable bequests would be made for business advantage, and while this is clearly a most important issue, it is a different one from that with which we are here concerned, that is to say the justification of giving for *non-business* purposes.

Political donations were not included in our study since most directors with whom we discussed donations took the view that political donations were a matter of business expectations, although the boards of some large companies consider that political donations should not be made. In the absence of shareholders' objections, most boards which now make such donations are likely to continue to make gifts to political parties or other organizations pledged to the support of private enterprise, notwithstanding the legal requirement, since January 1968, that political contributions must be disclosed in company accounts. A few boards are planning to obtain the formal consent of their shareholders to making political gifts. Shareholder opposition may be organized in future where Labour Party members and trades unionists hold shares, either directly or through investment trusts, in companies which contribute to the funds of the Conservative Party or to other organizations to which they are politically opposed. Some holders of units in the Trades Union Unit Trust are already indignant at the thought that they are contributing even in the smallest way to financing their political opponents.

Though there are some businessmen who have no doubt that it is positively their duty as officers of the company to allocate company funds to charitable donations, and others who are gravely doubtful of the legality and wisdom of so doing, the great majority of directors with whom we spoke and of companies included in our survey do sanction charitable donations though they appear hard put to it to explain very clearly the grounds for their decisions. Motives are mixed and objectives multiple in this as in other areas of business decision-making. But the significance of company donations is now such that some further efforts perhaps ought to be made to construct a more rational approach to the exercise of a board's responsibilities in this matter.

The total sum (£32 million in 1967) given annually by companies in the United Kingdom, and the size of individual grants (often £10,000–20,000) which account for three-quarters or more of funds raised by some appeals, are of an order which could be used to provide for significant developments in the community which are unlikely to attract public finance. Apart from independent foundations, given the present structure of taxation in Britain, companies are now the most likely source of sizeable gifts to charitable bodies, especially for capital developments.

It is possible to argue that companies ought not to be expected to make good the deficiencies of public funds for education, health and other elements of public welfare, and on these grounds some companies refuse to subsidize individual schools and hospitals. It is also possible to argue that the expectation of large industrial gifts inhibits the efforts which might otherwise be made by individuals and communities to raise their own funds, and some companies (more in the United States than in Britain), have tried to avoid this by offering to match funds raised from non-company sources. Nor can it be demonstrated that businessmen are any better judges than anyone else of which research, which charities or which artists ought to be sponsored at the expense of the shareholders, and by fiscal concessions.

From a company's point of view, many boards feel that they ought to be able to satisfy themselves that non-profit-seeking expenditure is made in a way which, in serving the public interest, serves the interests of the company at the same time. On this view it is perfectly proper for a company to weigh the effects of its giving upon the company's good name, upon its recruitment of staff, its relations with educational bodies and how its donations policy facilitates the general conduct of its business. This approach, which might be called a 'prudential'[1] theory of corporate giving, suggests that corporate philanthropy is a proper sphere of modern business activity and is similar to the kind of prudent long-term approach customarily applied to the investment of company income.

From the community's point of view, to encourage companies to make donations (as is done by tax concessions) not only has the advantage of generating additional funds for a variety of socially useful purposes, but it also enables independent institutions to survive and prosper in fields of education, social welfare and the arts for which 'no one could be so wise (or so foolish) as to try to devise uniform policies',[2] and for which, with present levels of taxation and other constraints on the accumulation of private fortunes, personal gifts are not likely to be sufficient.

Company donations could make a significant contribution to some contemporary social needs[3] and there would seem to be a strong case therefore for encouraging companies to adopt policies of innovative rather than merely responsive giving, in which industry provides the

[1] See R. Eells, 'A Philosophy of Corporate Giving', *The Conference Board Record*, New York, January 1968.

[2] F. Emerson Andrews, *Foundation Library Center Annual Report*, New York, 1967.

[3] If companies only raised their donations to 1 per cent of net income this would yield about the equivalent of one-quarter of the cost of all university education. (At present all private and corporate donations to universities contribute about 0.4 per cent of the universities' income.)

risk capital for independent institutions. This would mean that company boards would have to cease to regard donations as a necessary nuisance and the price of peace. Instead, businessmen would have to give the same kind of searching appraisal to the proposals of charitable societies which they give to business proposals. To develop a more positive and informed approach of this kind to donations without at the same time making unreasonable demands on company time requires some re-thinking about the best way to organize industrial giving both inside and outside companies.

While donations remain a small part of company funds (and if the present level were to be doubled, it would still amount to only 1 per cent of net profits), and in the absence of shareholders' objections, most boards are likely to treat company giving as an accepted business practice. They will, on the whole, give careful consideration to the exercise of their responsibilities for a mixture of business and non-business reasons which it is important to distinguish, even if where both kinds of reason are involved it may be fruitless to try to determine the exact proportions of self-interest and philanthropy in the mix.

If, however, demands were to be made for very much larger donations (for example in excess of 5 per cent of net income which is the limit for tax deductibility in the United States and some European countries) which, if met, would involve a level of expenditure of serious significance to the company's finances, boards might begin to feel that they had no mandate to pursue non-profit-seeking activities to this extent, and if they did not reach this conclusion themselves it might be pressed upon them by their shareholders. Similarly, if a higher level of company giving by covenants were to result in too great a loss of revenue, the desirability of encouraging company donations might be called into question, especially in so far as the creation of company trusts appeared to be motivated more strongly by a desire to keep control of companies in the hands of their existing owners than by charitable intentions.

Chapter 5

Case Study IV: Government Intervention; Protection of the Consumer and of the Public Interest

The supply and price of household detergents have been referred for examination twice by the Government: in 1963 to the Monopolies Commission, and in 1965 to the Prices and Incomes Board. The Prices and Incomes Board dealt only with the price reference and it was left to the more intensive study undertaken by the Monopolies Commission to consider whether the dominance of the market by two large companies and their expenditure on advertising and promotion might be against the public interest.

It is not surprising that the activities of these two companies were submitted to public scrutiny since they have between them so large a share of the market. Lever Brothers and Associates (wholly-owned subsidiary of Unilever) and Procter & Gamble (owned by the American Procter & Gamble Company) together supplied in 1965 about 85 per cent of hard soaps, 95 per cent of soap powders and flakes and synthetic laundry powders and well over half (63 per cent in 1964) of synthetic liquids. In toilet soaps, although Levers had at that time about 40 per cent of the market, the remainder was divided not only between Procter & Gamble and several other well known firms, but also among more than a hundred small producers. The total market was worth about £100 million per year in 1965, about 55 per cent of it soaps and soap flakes and powders and 45 per cent synthetic detergents.

The industry was referred to the Prices and Incomes Board because of price increases of between 8 and 12½ per cent in the year up to May 1965. The Board reported[1] that the increase in soap products was justified by increases in costs, but considered the increase in prices for synthetic powders was greater than was justified by the immediate movement in the costs of these products. The Board was generally

[1] National Board for Prices and Incomes, *Prices of Household and Toilet Soaps, Soap Powders and Soapless Detergents*, Cmnd. 2791, HMSO, 1965.

133

concerned with the difficulty of ensuring effective price competition, given the structure of this industry. In a market dominated by two major suppliers of approximately equal financial strength, price competition, it was believed, was limited because neither could gain a lasting advantage from it and in the detergents market consumer demand was not very sensitive to small price changes. The housewife, the Board believed, 'appears to be attracted by "special offers" of large but short-lived price reductions, by plastic daffodils, and dusters. But she is relatively impervious to smaller lasting price reductions or to a genuine addition to value for money such as is offered by bigger quantities for the same price.' The report accepted that companies had absorbed part of the increased costs of soap products and that this had eroded their profit margins, and that the prices of liquid synthetics had remained unchanged and in some cases been reduced by increasing the quantity per container. The report further accepted that there was competition, if not always price competition, in the industry and no collusion between the two major firms; that their management and industrial relations were good and that the companies were seeking to reduce administrative and distributional costs and generally to improve productivity. The cause for concern was that competition had been focused upon advertising and promotion and that selling expenses formed so high a part of costs, though even here the Board did not reject the companies' evidence that this kind of spending (in 1964 £8 million out of £9.25 million spent by the two companies on advertising was spent on television time) achieved high volume production and economies of scale in marketing. Nevertheless the Board considered that the amounts spent exceeded the level necessary to keep consumers informed of the choices available to them. Its recommendations were that prices should not be increased before the end of the following year and that recommended prices to retailers should cease. The companies felt able to accept these proposals, but they could not feel very happy at the doctrine which lay behind the Board's decision, which they complained seemed to assume that it was the duty of a company to absorb increased costs. If, and on the Board's own report this was held to be true, high profits were the result of efficient management, reducing them in this way, they protested, did not give companies much encouragement for further capital investment.

The Board did not pursue questions of market power and barriers against new entrants because the industry was already under review by the Monopolies Commission, which made its report the next year (August 1966). The main theme of this report also was the condemnation of expenditure, said to be excessive, on advertising and promotion. Competition in advertising was found to be the striking feature of this industry and an important element in its costs. The Commission pointed out that nearly a quarter of the final retail price paid by the consumer arose from the manufacturer's selling expenses, and they thought it most probable that what they considered exceptionally high advertising costs (11 per cent of retail prices in the case of Lever Brothers and 10 per cent in the case of Procter & Gamble) were a deterrent to new entrants to the industry. The report noted that the profits earned by Unilever (23.4 per cent in 1965 on historic cost basis, and 16.4 per cent on replacement cost basis), and by Procter & Gamble (53.2 per cent and 37 per cent respectively), were substantially above the average for manufacturing industry. Though both companies demonstrated that their prices had not increased as fast as the cost of living, the Commission criticized the escalation of selling costs resulting in concentration and promotion 'to the detriment of effective direct price competition and in unduly high profits[1] with the consequence that the public are charged unnecessarily high prices'.

The Commission's main recommendations were that there should be substantial percentage reductions in Unilever's and in Procter & Gamble's wholesale prices for household detergents and in their selling expenses, these reductions to be agreed with the Board of Trade. The order of these reductions should be not less that 40 per cent of selling expenses and 20 per cent average cut in prices. For the longer term, the Commission recommended that sanctions should be devised to prevent excessive selling expenditures in the field of household detergents.

The Commission's report was accepted immediately by the President of the Board of Trade[2] but its allegations as to excessive advertising costs and profits were vigorously refuted by the two major companies. They made it clear that they were not prepared voluntarily to implement the recommendations, and that if price reductions were imposed (especially if these were exclusive to the two companies), they would contest these. They did however offer to extend the price restraint accepted after the Prices and Incomes Board's earlier referral for another two years, and they offered some alternative pro-

---

[1] In this connection it has been pointed out that, unlike other investments, investment in advertising which also creates assets (consumer goodwill, etc.) is not added to the book value of the company, and, therefore, the *apparent* profits of companies which advertise heavily are higher owing to this accounting artifact. See J. H. Lorie, *Government and Advertising: The Heavy Hand of Benevolence*, University of Chicago, Selected Papers No. 27.

[2] But he later agreed to compromise on it. First he suggested a 15 per cent cut in prices to the companies. Then he agreed to a different arrangement. (See p. 138 below.)

posals to try to meet the objective which the Monopolies Commission had had in mind in its report.

In discussions with the Board of Trade, Unilever did not dispute that the company should take account of the public interest or indeed that there could be situations where they would agree to put this before the interests of their shareholders, but they did not accept that in this case the public interest was served by imposing a price reduction on their existing products. Five major assumptions of the Monopolies Commission were rejected by Unilever:

1 That the volume of their advertising was a result of, or calculated to, preserve their monopoly situation. Unilever pointed out that more is spent on advertising per £ of sales value in the liquids market than in the detergent market; yet there is more competition in the liquids market. The nearer a company is to a monopoly the less it needs to spend proportionately on advertising.

2 That advertising costs were excessive. Unilever argued that advertising is the cheapest method of selling this type of product, because the use of mass media economises on other intermediate selling expenses.

3 That profits were unduly high, being substantially above the levels of most manufacturing industry. Unilever contended that a fast growing technological industry ought to be earning profits above the average for all industries, which includes the performance of older declining industries.

4 That the level of advertising acted as a barrier to new entrants to the industry. Unilever pointed out that heavy brand advertising has not been found to be a barrier to small efficient firms in other industries, e.g. the tobacco industry. Nor in soaps and detergents has it prevented retailers like Sainsbury's or the Co-operative societies entering the market. Further if it is maintained that high advertising expenditure prevents the entry of smaller companies into the industry, the even higher selling costs which would be involved in replacing mass media advertising if this were undertaken would equally if not more effectively restrict entry.

5 That prices were unnecessarily high owing to factors like heavy advertising costs. Unilever claimed that prices were the lowest in Western Europe. They had not been increased for two years, since the undertaking given following the Prices and Incomes Board referral. Prices for these products rose less than the general rise in the retail price index between 1958 and 1965. Unilever maintained that the cheapest price is not the only consideration for the house-

wife. Supermarkets offer their own brands at lower prices than the major producers but they sell only to their own customers; they do not draw in a big clientele simply to buy cheaper soaps and detergents. Unilever had already for some years marketed an economy brand (Square Deal Surf) offering 18 per cent more powder in the packet for the standard price and it had gained only a small share of the market.

The company believed that the effect of the new price reductions of about 20 per cent, if imposed by the Board of Trade, would be the disappearance of Square Deal Surf (their economy brand) and probably some of the smaller British competitors. They also anticipated that the American company, Procter & Gamble, would be in a better position to withstand the reduction in profit margins expected to be an inevitable consequence of accepting the price reductions and would be likely to gain in market share with a consequent loss to Unilever's (and Britain's) export trade. Procter & Gamble would also be able to continue to draw on their much larger resources unrestricted in the United States while Unilever's basic 'power house' for product development in the UK would be hampered. The company would find it more difficult to attract capital since it could only earn a much less favourable return.

For these and many other reasons the company felt that, for a price reduction of, at most, 2d a week per household, the future development of the industry and its capacity to innovate and market new and better quality products was to be at the least retarded, if not seriously damaged. The advantages to be gained by the Commission's proposals seemed small and uncertain and the disadvantages certain and considerable.

The company however recognized that the President of the Board of Trade had a unanimous recommendation from the Monopolies Commission and considerable political pressure to act upon it, and they did not wish to refuse to be co-operative and to precipitate a confrontation with the Government: first, because the sight of a quasi-monopolistic giant company refusing to accept a unanimous government report that its advertising costs were excessive might create a very bad public image for the company; secondly, the company's experience of offering an economy brand made it confident that its own assessment of consumer reactions to cheaper brands was more likely to prove accurate than that of its critics. They therefore offered alternative proposals to widen the choice open to consumers for cheaper products marketed without expensive promotions, and finally both major companies agreed (April 1967) to offer a soap

137

powder, and a blue and a white synthetic detergent powder at a price 20 per cent below their current wholesale prices in each category. These were to be offered with all commercial marketing skill which would give consumers a genuine choice. The price of all reference products would remain unaltered for a further two years, when the Board of Trade would review the situation.

By this agreement the President was able to announce that a price reduction had been effected, that cheaper products would be available without expensive promotion, and that all prices referred would be kept at a standstill for another two years.

The companies had had to agree to offer more cheaper brands. (Unilever altered the basis of Surf from 18 per cent more in the packet to 20 per cent reduction in price and added a blue Surf powder and a new soap powder, Sunlight, to its economy range. Procter & Gamble reduced the price of its synthetic powder, Tide, and of its Oxydol soap powder by 20 per cent and added a blue Tide powder at a reduced price.)

But the companies did not have to make any reduction in the prices of their principal brands. They were satisfied that their market research equipped them better than the Board of Trade to judge consumer reaction to cheaper brands in competition with more heavily advertised products and they were confident of the outcome. The companies promised their co-operation in a study proposed by the President into the relation between advertising and competition, but were very doubtful about a proposal to explore the standardization of packaging for detergent products. Unilever did not like the insistence on price reduction instead of the extra powder content they had proposed for their Square Deal product (believing that the latter was a better marketing method) but agreed to accept this.

A year later (1968) all the 'economy' brands (six now instead of one), with some theme advertising but without any special promotion, had about 20 per cent of the market, which was only slightly larger than the share held before. (There had been no change in the quality of the cheaper powders but they had not of course had the same improvements incorporated in them as had been added to the more expensive and more heavily advertised brands.) It is difficult to interpret this result with any degree of certainty. Only one economy brand existed before and the additional economy packets were marketed under old well-publicised brand names and may have simply continued to attract the same customers. There was certainly no evidence of any substantial desertion by housewives to the cheaper brands. There seemed to be only a limited market among consumers for the lowest-priced washing powders. There were also other concurrent changes which might have influenced the market share of the economy brands. For example, partly because of retailers' price cuts and partly because of the temporary 'bargain pack' offers by manufacturers, the price of the more expensive brands was sometimes found to be cut, so that these could actually be bought for the same as the economy products. On the other hand, the effect of the Trade Descriptions Act may have tended to make retailers revert to recommended prices, which would leave a worthwhile saving to a consumer who chose economy packets. Also the decline of the market share of cheaper soap powders, which occurred over the same period, may be part of a continuing trend towards a decline in sales of all kinds of soap powders. But the most significant change has been the rapid development of new products with enzymes (Radiant and Ariel), which are substantially more expensive than both the standard brands and the economy packets. A penny or two on a packet or a plastic daffodil may not greatly influence some consumers but a difference in price of 1s or more must make the housewife seriously compare the price and quality of alternative washing agents. By May 1969 when the prices standstill ended, the position was much clearer and the trend unmistakable. The cheaper powders were showing a fall in their share of the market and the well publicized new brands with enzymes, despite their higher prices, were gaining steadily.

On the whole, this case of intervention essayed by the Board on behalf of the consumer public, while it achieved the objective of ensuring that the companies in question marketed a wider range of products at a lowered price made possible by the reduction of expenditure on advertising and promoting them, was not shown to be successful in interpreting consumer preferences. The Board's action did cause a wider range of economy brands to be made available to the housewife than had been offered before, but this has not proved attractive enough to detach very substantial numbers of customers from the more expensive brands. It is difficult to determine the effect of the Board's action on price levels. From April to December 1967 the average retail price of detergents (but not the price of the expensive brands) was lowered, and a number of reasons may have contributed to this. For example, the price of Surf was reduced immediately but packets containing 18 per cent more powder were sold until stocks were exhausted. The economy brands received much free publicity which put up their market share for two to three months to 25 per cent, and they were introduced with some kind of coupon or special offer which reduced their price by more than 20 per cent. Further, by December 1967 the effect of the price standstill was beginning to give the companies concern and both decided to end an agreement (a 'Code of Practice' relating to bargain packs and gifts), which had hitherto limited 'price off' promotions. Thereafter the more expensive brands were promoted by reduced price packets rather than free gifts and thus, though the market share of the economy brands was falling, the *average* retail price of all brands was below that in April 1967. It could be argued that the decision to end the agreement was influenced by the competitive pressure of the cheaper brands, but since the economy brands lost ground as soon as the more expensive enzyme products appeared on the market, it cannot be established whether competitive pressure from their lower price could have had any lasting influence on the price of other detergents. To the extent that prices were lowered this seems to have been the result of the decision to end the code-of-practice agreement, itself stimulated by the price standstill, though this can hardly have been a consequence intended by the Board which wanted more, not less, restriction on promotion and advertising. In the event the companies' overall expenditure on advertising (including expenditure on new enzyme products) has not been reduced as the Monopolies Commission had wanted, and the companies consider they have improved consumer choice and satisfaction by backing their business judgement that in the purchase of soaps and detergents the housewife would continue to be willing to pay for a higher priced product of her choice.

In sum, the British company in this case made it plain that they did not share the view that it was necessary for the Government to intervene in the public interest. This was not because of any rejection of the principle of government intervention in the public interest, but because board members felt that in this particular case that interest was best served by the producers' judgement of what the consumers wanted. The company did, however, co-operate with the Government, and two main reasons may be adduced for this. First, the relations of a company of this size with the Government cover a broad front, and board members might well judge that the company would lose more with respect to these relations as a whole than it could gain through a defiant attitude over this particular issue—quite apart from any ill effect that a row with the Government might have on the public's opinion of the company. Secondly, the company managed to work out, in co-operation with the Government, a scheme that would offer the consumer what the Government wanted, without placing a very great burden on the company. Thus the immediate costs of co-operation were not unduly heavy, while the costs of a refusal to co-operate might have been.

In this case, then, the company could be fairly satisfied with the outcome. But the equation may not always work out in this way, as may be seen from two further illustrations of occasions on which there has been official intervention, this time regarding mergers. Obviously mergers are another kind of business decision where it can be argued that because public interests may be involved the outcome cannot simply be left to a trial of strength between the companies concerned.

In January 1969 two proposed mergers, the first between Unilever and Allied Breweries and the second between Rank and De La Rue, were referred to the Monopolies Commission since they involved the elimination of separate enterprises with assets of over £5 million (Section 6, Monopolies and Mergers Act 1965). The Commission reported in June 1969 and found that in the first case a merger was not likely to operate against the public interest, but in the second case it recommended that a merger should not be permitted. The reasons given for these two decisions were accompanied by some 'General Observations on Mergers' with special reference to the development of 'conglomerates'.

In the case of Unilever/Allied Breweries the commission applied the conventional tests as to the possibility of consequences inimical to the public interest. In relation to the effects on concentration, barriers to new entrants, anti-competitiveness due to resources being able to be deployed among a number of products with the possibility of using one sector to subsidize unprofitable prices in another, and the control of outlets, the Commission were satisfied that no significant disadvantages would accrue. They believed there were indications that there could be gains in marketing and technical efficiency, and possibly that competition would be stimulated among other large brewers. On the grounds advanced as most important by the companies themselves, i.e. the possibility of developing an international drinks business which would be favourable to UK exports, the Commission thought the public benefits seemed 'small and uncertain' but they recognized the need of a company like Unilever Limited to keep a balance between its activities and profits in the UK and those of its associated company Unilever NV in the Netherlands, and they gave a rather lukewarm approval to the merger. By this time (June 1969) the market's assessment of the two companies' shares had changed in such a way as to discourage further moves towards a merger and the proposals were dropped. It remains to be seen whether or how Unilever will make any further efforts to enter the international brewing business (e.g. by the acquisition of a Continental brewery company based on Unilever NV), and whether this will prove an avoidable loss to the British economy unless alternative and equally profitable uses for these resources are found. If so the need for the company to await the approval of the Monopolies Commission might be said to have worked in the long run against the public interest.

The second case concerned a contested bid by the Rank Organization for De La Rue, and the Commission recommended that this be refused mainly on the grounds that the senior management of De La Rue would leave the organization, and that this would gravely prejudice the company's business, especially its important overseas connections, which could not be made good quickly by Rank because of the difference in the character of their businesses. It did not find any important grounds on which the merger would be harmful to competition, but, despite this, thought that the bid should not be permitted.

This second decision raises a number of important issues. In the first place, the managements of other companies faced with a take-over may be encouraged to try to frustrate it by the threat of an exodus of top management with consequent damage to the company's organization and business connections. In the second place, the Commission flatly rejected the right and competence of the shareholders and their advisers to judge the efficiency aspects of a takeover.

'In the first place, and this is especially true of contested mergers, the Commission may, and probably will, have more information than the market on which to base an assessment of the likely outcome. Secondly, we have to reckon with the fact that shareholders faced with an offer are more likely to be concerned with its financial implications for themselves, including tax considerations, than with the efficiency with which resources are to be used. We conclude that the Stock Market's reaction cannot therefore be relied on to reflect the efficiency aspects of a takeover.'

This was a frank statement of doubt about the shareholder's knowledge of his own interest, and indeed the whole tone of the report represents the very reverse of what Lord Goodman has called the 'cult of the shareholder'. (The Commission made no criticism of the voting structure of Rank which did not give control to the equity holders.) Can a distinction be made between the financial implications for shareholders and the efficient use of resources in this way?[1] Shareholders and their advisers can certainly be mistaken in their judgements but what reason is there to suppose that they will be more prone to error than the Commission or other government agencies? Where the public interest, for example in matters of defence, the

[1] See also *The Times*, 16 June 1969.

balance of payments, etc., might be adversely affected by the scale or nature of a proposed merger, governments will have a duty to intervene and try to determine whether a merger, conglomerate or otherwise, ought to be allowed to proceed. However, these are quite different grounds on which to give or withhold approval from that advanced as a general background to the decision in the Rank case where the Commission claimed that it was better informed, and thus better able to judge a contested takeover bid, than the market.

Chapter 6

The Case Studies: a Summary

Three of the four cases studied were concerned with examining the voluntary efforts of companies to act in what they themselves believed to be a socially responsible way, and these exhibited some common features. By contrast the fourth case concerned a company board where an external, and to the company unacceptable, interpretation of social responsibility was imposed upon it.

In the first three cases it was clear that to pioneer developments in employee relations or to make company donations was congenial to most of the senior management, and this was broadly true for all companies with whom this was discussed. These activities are a source of pride and satisfaction to many company boards. The prestige of being a leading company in an industry is often linked with innovations in industrial welfare and munificent company gifts, and in part these policies which are identified as socially responsible may be an investment in 'management ego'. Though some directors complained and others emphasized that the burden was not of their seeking, few wished to be relieved of the responsibility of deciding upon the scale and destination of company gifts, and many senior members of company boards concerned themselves closely with employee welfare. One reason why boards undertake these non-profit-seeking activities may simply be because their members like it.[1]

The extension of state welfare and the greater affluence of some workers have sometimes led to the suggestion that the responsibility of industry to provide occupational benefits, funds to support education, etc., is no longer so pressing and that even if these obligations cannot be reduced they need not be further extended in the future. Companies in this enquiry, however, expected and accepted that they were likely to have more rather than fewer responsibilities in industrial welfare and community action in the future. They believed that the additional money provided by company donations towards the support of education, charities, and the arts would continue to be sought after to supplement public funds, and that, because it is con-

[1] Chapter 3 above. See also W. G. McClelland, *The Creation of Wealth and its Distribution*, The Industrial Co-partnership Association, 1968.

venient to organize social benefits around people's places of employment, other occupationally-related schemes (e.g. employee saving schemes) were likely to be set up. Further, they pointed out some emerging social problems which will require the active co-operation of employers to solve them, e.g. preventing racial discrimination in the provision of jobs and training.

The extent to which individual companies provided above-average fringe benefits, protected amenities and made charitable donations, etc., did not seem to correlate closely with company size (i.e. by assets) or with profit records. With respect to charitable donations on the average the very large companies and the very small companies gave less proportionately than medium-sized and large companies (see p. 113 above) and some companies gave donations even when they made a loss. (This may be because they are committed to payments under a covenant undertaken in more prosperous days.) Some companies of all sizes, ranging from ICI to small family firms, have some form of profit sharing and/or co-partnership. It has been suggested[1] that in America developing new ways of expressing the social purpose of a business tends to be linked with an above-average level of competitive and innovative activity in a company, that is, a firm which is sensitive to other kinds of market change is likely to be the first to respond to changing public expectations about business behaviour. This was certainly true of some of the companies which co-operated in this enquiry but not enough data were collected about British companies to substantiate any general conclusion of this kind.

This study was concerned with how company boards themselves viewed the concept of social responsibility and how they described their business behaviour in this respect. Representatives of employees with whom this was discussed were less enthusiastic about some of these policies, and some were frankly sceptical. Some union representatives believed that social responsibility was just another name for an approach to workers' interests now out of fashion, namely paternalism, and that despite changes of nomenclature some of the policies which companies called socially responsible came very near to thrusting upon employees the management's image of loyal co-operative servants of the company unreservedly committed to the company's objectives. Participation in management and even, in some cases, security of employment were not so highly prized by employees as might have been expected, or at any rate did not take precedence over other conditions which they would have preferred employers to make available. So long as these efforts to be socially

[1] Orace Johnson, Corporate Philanthropy, *Journal of Business*, University of Chicago, October 1966.

145

responsible emanate from board rooms or the higher ranks of management, they will tend to be received with some caution by those who represent workers' interests. In the company studied here which was evolving a more participative style of management the initiative for this development and its continuance did come from the company, but they appreciated that sustained efforts were necessary to associate employees and their representatives with company policy, and the productivity bargains which were finally negotiated did seem to represent a genuine conjunction of company and employee's interests.

'Another stumbling block was the workers' invincible mistrust of the possibility of a manager having any other aim than that of robbing them as much as possible. They were firmly convinced that his real aim (whatever he might say) would always be hidden in what he did not tell them. And they themselves when they talked, said much, but never what they really wanted. Besides all this the workers put as the first and unalterable condition in any agreement that they should not be obliged to use any new methods or new kinds of tools for their work. When talking to the workers and explaining to them the advantages of co-partnership he felt that they were only listening to the sound of his voice and were quite determined, whatever he might say, not to let themselves be taken in. He felt this especially when talking to the most intelligent of them.'[1]

Modern managers are only too familiar with some of these sentiments, and perhaps this is why some company spokesmen were less than forthright in distinguishing the motives for their social policies. Some hesitated to talk too openly about the business pay-off which was expected and seemed to think that a calculating attitude to welfare would destroy the credibility of the company's attempt to be socially responsible and would not improve industrial relations. Others protested rather more than the facts seemed to justify that all their policies were wholly dictated by unalloyed profit-seeking. Though motives are always likely to be mixed, concepts of social responsibility for companies would be less confusing if companies costed their social policies, whether considered from the point of view of a social duty or a business pay-off or both. Resources allocated to social purposes, or policies undertaken for social as well as business reasons, are rarely subsequently scrutinized for their effec-

---

[1] Leo Tolstoy, *Anna Karenina*, 1875, quoted in *Workers' Participation in Industry*, J. Ward Daw, 1968.

tiveness in the way in which other kinds of business investment are examined. The company in this study whose efforts to provide security of employment were examined made significant changes in its policies after studying the analysis of the cost and effectiveness of its policy.

The company which was enjoined to alter the marketing of its products in the interests of its consumers was similar to the other companies studied in respect of *voluntary* social policies, i.e. it made generous company donations (some being given in advance of requests for assistance as part of a positive company policy) and set itself very high standards of working conditions and fringe benefits for its employees, but in general these policies were considered to be part of intelligent management undertaken for good business reasons. The company did not reject the idea that businesses may be required to yield their own to the public interest under certain circumstances, and that they must pursue their business activities with due regard for their impact upon the community as a whole. They did, however, find it difficult to accept the official view that they were not serving the consumer interest, when this view ran contrary to their own assessment based upon extensive business experience and market research. The problem of defining social responsibility in a way which can, if necessary, be legally enforced, is, of course, very different from the evolution of a public expectation regarding the responsible policies towards employees, consumers and the community at large that companies should follow of their own accord. In general the case studies illustrate both some of the difficulties which can face companies that deliberately aim at social responsibility as a company objective, and at the same time show some developments of considerable value to employees and to the community which arise from such attempts.

The approach to social responsibility displayed in these case studies and accepted by the companies consulted would, however, be dismissed as very narrow by some critics of company boards because these developments were largely initiated by managements and did not seem to make very much difference to the overall control of the companies. If, on the other hand, the social responsibility of companies is taken to imply that interests other than those of shareholders should have equal consideration and representation, this would obviously involve a much greater change in the relations of company boards with organized labour and with government than anything which has yet arisen from employee welfare schemes or company philanthropy, or even from participative management of the kind evidenced in this study, which still left the initiative for major decisions of company policy to the board. Approaches to social responsibility, whether as a form of good management practice or as a different distribution of power in the company involving changes in company law, are often explained in terms of the concept of balancing interests, and this prescription for company policy deserves a more critical scrutiny than it usually receives.

Chapter 7

A Note on Balancing Interests

It has been noted in the preceding chapters that the concept of the balance of interests has a wide appeal both to independent observers of the company scene and to company directors themselves. Indeed, on first consideration, striving to balance interests sounds a very reasonable way of trying to resolve conflicts and, moreover, seems to correspond with what company boards think they are doing when they exercise business judgement. There is, however, a good deal of confusion about what is meant by balancing interests. For example, does this mean resolving conflicts by a compromise which concedes some of the claims of all interested parties, or does it mean acting in such a way as to cause their interests to coincide? Coincidence and balance are very different concepts. Two interests coincide when each is served by the other or when they are served in common by some act or policy. They are balanced against each other when each is adjusted in order to meet the claims of the other.

As is shown in this chapter, what is seen in the short term as a compromise where two interests are balanced, for example when a wage increase is negotiated, may well serve the interests of both parties—employees and shareholders—in the long run. But whether a particular short-run compromise will make for a long-run co-incidence of interests will frequently be a matter of business judgement rather than of ascertainable fact. For the practical purpose of managerial decision-taking, this presents no problem; indeed, most important business decisions are based on such judgements rather than on certainty. In this chapter, however, we are considering the implications of the balance-of-interest concept for the law rather than for day-to-day management decision-taking; and in this context, when we try to establish precisely what are the interests to be balanced and what kind of balance ought to be sought, the difficulties involved in trying to embody these ideas either in law or in codes of company practice are at once apparent.

The major interests to be considered are, but not in any order of importance, consumers, creditors, workers, the nation or the public as a whole (in the form of the 'public interest'), and shareholders.

149

Consumers

Let us take first the case of consumers' interests. Clearly it should be the purpose of business to serve the needs of consumers, but in what sense and for what reasons ought the interests of consumers to be balanced against other interests? In what ways may the interests of consumers conflict with those of the other claimants to the proceeds of economic activity?

In the cases of shareholders and creditors it is unnecessary to balance their interests against those of consumers if, and to the extent that, long-run profit is maximized by optimum attention to consumers' needs, for in such circumstances they would coincide. Hence the question which arises here is what should be the principles of policy where long-run profit is maximized by some divergence from the optimum satisfaction of consumers' needs. In the cases of workers and the nation or public, there may at all times be a measure of conflict of interest between them and consumers. Workers' interests and the 'public interest' in the conduct and proceeds of business are of a more complex character than those of shareholders and consumers. They comprehend wider areas and purposes than those upon which shareholders and consumers might focus their attention, and hence the possibility of conflict and the need for balance are, at least at first sight, more likely to arise.

First then we may consider how a conflict of interest may arise because long-run profit is maximized by some divergence from the optimum satisfaction of consumers' needs. This may arise either because producers have a measure of monopolistic market power, or because consumers' demands do not accurately reflect their needs.

In the first of these two cases, there is certainly a place for measures to reduce or remove monopoly power. Where such measures are taken by the State, they become part of the framework of law within which business should operate, not objectives of company boards to be put in the balance against other objectives. Hence the concept of balance can come into play only in so far as, in addition to the role of law in this field, there is also a role for discretionary action by company boards. Their discretion is, moreover, frequently exercised on commercial rather than social grounds. Thus those companies which restrain their expansion lest they become objects of anti-monopolist action (e.g. giant companies which already hold a very large part of their markets), may strike a commercial balance between the advantages of expansion (and thus their shareholders', and perhaps their consumers' interests) and the disadvantages of hostile state or public action. There are also companies which hold a monopolistic (or oligopolistic) position but refrain from taking full, or any, advantage of it against their consumers. Here too the boards balance the advantages against the disadvantages of the exploitation of a monopoly position, and here again, while a company may exercise restraint on grounds of social responsibility and not because it would lose commercially by failing to do so, the balance may again be struck on clearly commercial grounds.

If for example a company refrains from seeking or exploiting monopoly power for fear of undesirable *business* reactions (e.g. the entry of new competitors), it is a case of a business decision which, like many others, affects the company's success, and has no need to call in aid a theory of balance between shareholder's and consumer's interests. If its restraint arises from a fear of inviting hostile legal or administrative action, it is in essence a case of observing the constraints of the framework of law and acting within them. Such action may have harmful effects for consumers, shareholders and indeed the public (e.g. where an efficient company follows a policy of 'live and let live' with less efficient competitors for fear of inviting anti-monopoly action), but this raises a question of the propriety of the framework of law. Defects in the framework of law may or may not be remediable. If they are, then the remedy ought to be supplied by the law or by public administrative action. If they are not, it must be because no suitable rule to cure the defect has yet been devised. In that case the 'balance of interests' implies no more than the use of judgement about a company's social responsibilities, and should not be taken to mean that there can be a precise code for company boards—for those who try to draw it up will encounter the same difficulties as those whose task it is to shape and maintain the framework of law.

It may perhaps be contended that anti-monopoly law and administration are properly to be viewed as machinery whereby the State, as distinct from company boards, enforces a balance between shareholders' and consumers' interests. But the purpose of such law and administration should be to make these interests as nearly as possible coincide, not balance; and a concept of balance is not relevant in so far as this purpose is fulfilled.

The second case of possible divergence between shareholders' and consumers' interests, i.e. that which may arise because consumers' demands may not accurately represent their needs, raises complex problems of consumer behaviour. On the one hand there are clearly imperfections in consumers' knowledge of their needs and how they may be satisfied, and there is no doubt that in assessing their needs they are influenced by the persuasions of producers. On the other hand consumers are in large measure aware of the various alternatives open to them, do discriminate in their purchases, and can often tell where the persuasions of producers are not substantially matched by the suitability of the goods or services offered.

There are numerous ways in which consumers' knowledge and powers of independent judgement can be improved which are outside the purview of company boards, for example by consumer organization, independent testing of products, the sale of information concerning rival products, the establishment of standards by governmental or independent private bodies. The question to be considered here is whether there is any kind of balance which ought properly to be struck by company boards. Where a board acts with integrity in its dealings with consumers and with a concern for their welfare beyond what they would themselves independently demand, but does so with an eye to the long-run maximization of profits, again it is a case of coincidence, not of balance, of interests. But there are no doubt cases where a special concern for the welfare of consumers runs counter to long-run profit. Ought company boards in such cases to trim their shareholders' interests in some measure to effect a balance with consumers' interests? Suppose, for example, that the demand for cars seems to reflect a preference for cheapness rather than safety. If this arises because purchasers underestimate the true cost of the risks to *themselves* in sub-optimally safe cars, producers may in the interests of long-run profit spend money to apprise them of the true facts, and if producers do this there is again a case of coincidence, not balance. But suppose that the car purchasers do not underestimate the cost of the risks to themselves, but disregard the cost of the risks to others (pedestrians, other motorists, taxpayers, etc.). Ought then the producers to give the consumers not what they demand but what it is believed they ought to have? There is clearly a very strong case for doing so. But in general the balance both of social and of economic advantage would seem to lie where producers see themselves as the servants, not the masters, of consumers. If consumers seek what it is socially disadvantageous for them to seek, the remedies must surely preponderantly take the form of social action; action by producers is not likely to be sufficient, for their perspective is unlikely to be exactly right for such purposes.

Creditors

In this context creditors' interests are of a narrower character than the other interests with which we are concerned. Creditors need to be protected against fraud and recklessness in the use of company assets. This raises questions for the reform of company law, and provisions desirable from this point of view may hobble the power of directors to serve non-creditor interests. But it is usually only in the short run and to a partial extent that this can be said to raise a question of balance between creditor and non-creditor interests. As long as it is borne in mind that creditors cannot be insulated from risk and that directors must have room for manoeuvre as businessmen to be successful, the long-run interests of creditors approximately coincide with those of others except perhaps where a decision to wind up a company is in question. Where there is some doubt about its future viability shareholders, and even more employees, may prefer to take whatever chance there is of future success and hold on, whereas creditors will be likely to want the company to be wound up if its assets would still pay off their claims.

Workers

It is in the consideration of workers' interests that the more difficult problems of balance arise. If one thinks only of remuneration, there is a substantial degree of coincidence between workers' *long-run* interests and the *long-run* interests of others within the conventional wage system. For despite the great imperfections of the labour market which produce numerous anomalies (geographical immobility, imperfect knowledge of job opportunities, 'non-competing groups', discrepancies between strong and weak unions or employers associations and between unionized and non-unionized labour), and despite the injury to other interests which may possibly be caused by, for example, wage-push inflation, over the long run workers' remuneration proceeds hand in hand with industrial profitability as a yardstick of efficiency, the service of consumer needs, and the general expansion of the economy. Still, the coincidence is certainly not perfect even in the long run, so that the question of profit-sharing arises, and in the short run there can be a sharp conflict between workers' remuneration and the interests of shareholders and consumers. Furthermore, remuneration is not the workers' only interest. They have an interest in the conditions of their work, and also in the processes of managerial decision-making. As far as conditions of work are concerned, it is possible to treat them as in the nature of fringe benefits and therefore as an element of remuneration (of course there are numerous differences between wages, regular fringe benefits, and the value of good or bad conditions of work, especially in their distribution and their bases of settlement, but these are mainly irrelevant in this context). But in the case of the processes of managerial decision-making, there are two questions to be considered. First, since workers clearly have an interest in them, does this interest establish a claim to participation in decision-making (that is to say, over and above the ways in which

153

workers already participate in different firms and countries, e.g. partly negatively, partly positively, partly unilaterally)? Secondly, do boards have powers, and if not, should they have them, to consider the interests of employees beyond what may be necessary for business? The matters which must be considered here are:

(a) questions of short-run balance,
(b) profit-sharing as an element in long-run balance, and
(c) participation in management and its control.

In the short run, workers may gain an advantage against share-holders or consumers, and *vice versa*. The situation will be determined by the state of the labour market, itself governed by the extent and character of trade-union power and employers' power, the state of the market for shareholders' capital, and the degree of competition in the markets for the workers products. These are all institutional and environmental factors which present problems for public policy, but in the short run only marginally for company boards in the form of a need to balance interests. Where trade-union power is strong, boards have limited room for manoeuvre. Where their room for manoeuvre is considerable, they have a choice between some measure of profit, of better service to consumers, or of better remuneration (in the widest sense) to the workers; and in this sense it is true that they have to make a balance of interests. But it is another matter to formulate it into a set of rules that could be enforced in the courts; and although such a balancing of interests is always taking place, boards are doing this within the framework of the existing law. In this sense, the balancing of interests need only mean that shareholders' interests are to be served with due regard to the calls for fair and generous dealing in all human relationships, such as would also apply to individuals dealing with each other, to the trustees of charities dealing with their employees, and to the State dealing with its employees. In all these cases certain interests other than those of the workers are paramount in law, but they ought to be served in a manner consistent with some canon of good conduct. Of course the measure of fairness or generosity of employees will not be the same in all cases. An individual disposing of his own property, a board directing the affairs of a company, a trustee managing the resources of a charity, are not in the same position and do not have the same power of right to exercise generosity to employees. Hence the canons of good conduct will not be precisely the same in all cases.[1] Standards

---

[1] The case of fair or generous dealing with employees should be distinguished from generosity to third parties. A company board may well take the view that whereas individuals ought to give to charities, such donations are not a proper

of industrial conduct can of course be the subject of industrial legislation and the law can be amended from time to time to take account of new expectations and demands, but these are then related to specific rights and obligations for employers and employees. Company boards will often go beyond this in seeking to serve what they believe to be the employees' interests—although the results of the case study on improving security of employment in the building industry (Chapter 2) show that care must be taken to ensure that such policies do in fact serve the employees' interests.

The idea that workers should share in profits as an element in the long-run balance of interests rests mainly upon the footing that wages and fringe benefits do not measure up to the full value of the workers' contribution to output.[1] If the 'full value' of the workers' contribution means its market value, the machinery for measuring it is the wage market, and profit-sharing is not needed to enable the market to determine it. If the workers' market power is too weak, so that they receive less than their marginal product value, the remedy must be to strengthen it, and this is the view normally taken by trade unions and the majority of the workers. If their market power is too strong, so that unemployment or wage-push inflation results, then whatever the remedy may be, it is not likely to be profit-sharing. If 'full value' means not market value but some other quantity assessed by an arbitration board, a wage council, a Prices and Incomes Board, or some similar body, what is at issue is here also the proper magnitude of a wage, and this is normally established without recourse to any profit-sharing devices.

In a less simple form the argument for profit-sharing sometimes rests upon the proposition that the worker 'invests' his career in his employment and that the market takes no account of this in the process of wage determination. Is this correct? First, it may be argued that it is not true that the market takes no account of this 'investment' in wage-making, though whether it does so adequately raises the possibly unanswerable question of what is adequate. Secondly, on the view that profit is a residual, it is hard to see why the remuneration for this 'investment' should take the form of a share of a fund of such

---

use of company funds (unless a business return is expected, in which case the motive is not charitable). See Chapter 4, 'Company Giving'.

[1] Alternatively it could rest upon the proposition that it is a fairer or more effective system of renumeration. If it is fairer it must mean that wages should vary with the risks of the business as do profits. The view that the workers should thus shoulder part of the risks by way of a fluctuating income would however seem to be acceptable to very few, at least in Britain. The proposition that profit-sharing may be a more effective system is considered below.

a nature. Shareholders take their pay in the form of a share of this residual (if we accept at this point this view of the nature of profit) because they alone are not entitled to contractual pay, as the workers, managers, and the suppliers of loan capital are. There is no reason in principle why workers should not hire all the other factors of production contractually (including the capital now provided by the shareholders), and take the residual themselves. There are cases where this happens, but it normally does not, because workers are not in a position to take the risks involved. Instead they are hired contractually by others who take the risks of residual pay, namely the shareholders. If one takes the alternative view that in practice in most public companies dividends are viewed by the managers as quasi-contractual, and that it is not the shareholders who hire the managers but the managers who hire the other factors of production, including the shareholders' capital,[1] it still does not follow that the 'full value' of the workers' contribution to output needs to be assessed in a partly variable form rather than a fixed form. On either view there appears to be no link between the workers' career 'investment' and entitlement to residual pay.

Of course managers may well decide in the pursuit of profit that the interests of the business in a co-operative labour force are served by paying the workers part of the residual. But this is less a case of balancing the shareholders' or the managers' interests against workers' interests, than an attempt to cause them to coincide.

Proposals for worker participation in management rest either upon the proposition that it is the workers' right or upon the view that it enhances the efficiency of business and thus increases the social product. The claim of right may rest upon the contention that the worker 'invests' his career in the business which has been discussed above, or upon some more broadly based value judgements about industrial democracy. The other argument for participation is that of efficiency, and increasingly managements are becoming convinced that this is true in so far as participation is taken to mean the greater involvement of company employees at all levels in the planning and organization of the company's business. There is not yet much firm evidence of a general kind on this, but a number of individual companies believe that their efforts to increase direct participation and consultation among their staff have added greatly to their satisfaction and productivity.[2] If, however, it is assumed that management is ultimately in the hands of the board, it may be contended that true participation must involve some share in the power of the board and employees must be represented upon it. The crucial question is, whose

[1] See below.   [2] See Chapter 4 above.

interests are the workers' board representatives to serve? Is it to be the workers' interests or the interests of the business generally? If it is to ensure that the interests of the workers are properly examined and understood, participation on the board would seem to be a lower priority than an effective system of consultation, works committees and competent personnel administration, etc. If it is to be the interests of the business generally, how would appointment to the board by the workers add to efficiency? Perhaps by engendering loyalty and content-ment among the workers; but any such effect is likely to be limited because it is probable that, if there is a gulf between the board and the workers, it will also arise between the workers and their own appoin-tees on the board, as long as these appointees have to serve the interests of the business and not the special interest of the workers. British companies in this study which have had experience through their European connections of workers' representation on boards have not found that this had any significant influence upon their deliberations.

The 'Public Interest'

What is described as the public interest comprehends a wide variety of matters. It includes some aspects of the interests of consumers, creditors, workers, and shareholders; but here we are concerned with matters outside the fields of these groups. To a substantial extent they concern the framework of law within which business must operate, and do not raise problems for company behaviour, other than the need to conform to the law, and perhaps the desirability of improving upon it. Smoke control, the discharge of effluent, the location of industry, regional planning, and the control of monopoly and restrictive practices, are examples of matters of this kind. It is true that, if, as many have done in the past, companies improve upon the law, acting as pioneers for the development of the law, a problem arises of reconciliation with the interests of consumers, creditors, workers and shareholders. However, such cases are often those where practice beyond the requirements of the law is developed in such a way that its long-run effects are expected to be beneficial to the company, if only in the sense that a failure to do these things will, by offending social expectations about business behaviour, create a hostile environment for business activity.

The cases where the framework is not legal but conventional (e.g. codes for takeover bids) are not in essence dissimilar. The problems which arise are still concerned with rules to be obeyed, not with ends which may be chosen in whole or in part or not at all and which, if chosen, must be balanced against other ends.

The kind of case which does go to the heart of the matter on

157

balancing interests is that arising from national economic policies which are not embodied in law or quasi-law at all, and which is not intended to make a part of the framework of business law. Thus calls by governments to export, or to hold down prices, wages, or dividends, where such action conflicts with business advantage, produce cases of this kind. To what extent ought company boards to heed such calls when the result, at least in the short run and possibly also in the long run, must be inimical to all the interests which they normally expect to serve? Here there appears to be a genuine problem of balance.

There are three major approaches to the problem of this kind of case. First, governmental exhortations may be ignored or rejected, on the ground that the Government should either embody its desires in law or keep silent upon them. To exhort business to do things contrary to its view of its interests but not required by law is to seek the power of law without going through the process of law-making. In defence of law itself and the rights of citizens, it may be said, such exhortation should be rejected.

Secondly, the case may simply be an example of the familiar conflict between short-run and long-run interests. For example, exports may be unprofitable for a particular firm, but if its exports help to safeguard the stability and progress of the economy, gain will accrue to it. The case where all will gain if all act in a certain way, but where the gain cannot arise if each seeks his own immediate advantages, is a variation of this. On this view of the Government's 'public interest' guide-lines, the problem for company boards is not difficult in principle, though it may be in practice. It is a matter of business judgement to balance short-run against long-run gain or gain from community action against gain from individual action.

Thirdly, the public interest may be permanently opposed to the interests normally served by business, and therefore it may call for lasting sacrifice by business; yet the sacrifice is expected to be made voluntarily, not by compulsion of law. In this case company boards must balance the sacrifice against the other interests, but on what basis can they assess the extent of the sacrifice to be made? The answer appears to be that there is no basis except judgement about what may be called a balance of interests but which would certainly be hard to reduce to a set of stipulations precise enough to be incorporated usefully in the company law.

There is a further point about the 'public interest' which must be noted. There may be as many views of the public interest as there are members of the public, and it may not be universally accepted that the Government's view, unless and until it is embodied in law, should be accepted in preference to any other. As Professor Fogarty has pointed out 'continental jurists have wrestled for years with the problem of giving a positive content to the notion that firm has an obligation to the public interest. They have ended by agreeing practically unanimously that though this concept has value for indicating a general direction to which firms should look, it cannot be usefully defined so as to lay on them a precise legal obligation to do this or that.'[1] Deciding that the nationalized industries are to be run for and on behalf of the public as a whole has not provided the corporations with any clear set of rules to guide them in decisions about the maintenance of uneconomic services, expenditure on the protection of amenities and similar matters.

Shareholders
Attitudes to the interests of shareholders vary according to views upon the extent of their paramountcy and these in turn vary according to views upon the role of shareholders. If they are regarded as the same as debenture holders or other lenders of capital, except that their remuneration is not contractually fixed, they will not be treated as the owners of companies, whatever the legal form may lay down. Alternatively, even if they are regarded as rightful owners, the interests of others (consumers, workers, the nation) may be judged to take precedence over certain of the rights of ownership. Or, thirdly, the practical difficulties in the way of organizing genuine shareholders' control and the apathy of shareholders themselves may lead to the conclusion that it is idle to seek to maintain a system in which shareholders are invested with the rights of owners. On the other hand, the position may be defended that shareholders are, and ought to be, treated as owners, and that company law and practice should be reformed to make their ownership effective.

Some of these concepts of the company which do not recognize shareholders as owners would leave effective ownership with management (the 'self-perpetuating oligarchies' of some critics of the system), or with management-cum workers where there is worker participation. The result in either case tends to be pressure for State control which in large measures amounts to State ownership. Yet this is not the result which is desired by most of those who are opposed to the present system of what they feel to be ineffective shareholder ownership.

However, the kinds of solution which are put forward by reformers who would like to dethrone the shareholder and bring the influence of other groups to bear on the management of a company's affairs depend upon accepting the concept of the 'balance of interests' as a

[1] M. Fogarty, *A Companies Act, 1970?* PEP, 1969.

basis for reformed company law, about which a number of objections have been noted above. This would apply to the idea of a supervisory board,[1] if such a body were composed equally of representatives of various interest groups (workers, consumers, shareholders etc.), especially if members had powers to intervene in the executive management of the company, 'though it could be argued that institutional rather than legal changes could be introduced to give effect to the representation of other interests alongside shareholders, with fewer difficulties'. Minority representatives, e.g. one worker director, on the other hand are unlikely to have a very significant influence. A supervisory board which was in effect a shareholder's committee would be a quite different proposition and, if the aim is to make shareholder control as an ultimate sanction really effective, there is much to be said for some arrangement of this kind. However the emphasis of such a committee would be likely to be on efficiency rather than social responsibility.

Company boards always state that it is their duty to serve the shareholders' interests (some consider it to be the special responsibility of 'outside' directors to safeguard the shareholders), but in companies not under the close control of their owners the board very often consists of senior executives who are heads of departments and very much orientated to management interests.

The question might be asked how could shareholders be persuaded to vote for a shareholders' committee when they neglect to use their present powers to elect the board itself? Whatever reforms of company law and practice are evolved which bring the shareholder's position closer to that of an effective owner, e.g. greater disclosure of the facts of the company's business, it would be foolish to expect to find a way of inducing the majority of shareholders (though not perhaps those with the majority of *shareholdings*) to take an active interest in the affairs of their companies, except in the case of the closely controlled companies where they already do so. Why are the general body of private (i.e. non-institutional) shareholders apparently so apathetic about their investments? Is it because theirs is, as one observer[2] has called it, a 'well-nourished' apathy, i.e. shareholders are well satisfied as long as a company appears to be successful and only become active when the difficulties of the company can no longer be concealed and when it may be too late to prevent serious losses? Most shareholders appear to have neither time nor inclination

[1] For a discussion of the supervisory board as used in Germany see M. Fogarty, *A Companies Act* 1970?, PEP, Broadsheet No. 500, 1969.
[2] F. R. Jervis, *The Company, The Shareholder, and Growth*, Hobart Paper, No. 37, Institute of Economic Affairs.

to read company accounts and attend meetings. Even those well able to understand a balance sheet expect to depend on professional investment advice in the same way that they use other specialist services such as that of tax accountants to deal with their affairs; in these cases it may be not so much lack of interest as lack of time. Failure to use them is not in itself a reason for removing the powers of shareholders; the individual voter is just as powerless as the individual shareholder and he can call his managers to account only once in five years. His opportunities for understanding the complexities of the affairs with which his government has to deal might appear no greater than that of the shareholder who is trying to pierce the corporate veil. One great difference between them is that the elector has at least a vigilance committee, the official Opposition, who comment upon and question the day-to-day conduct of public affairs and relentlessly pursue any evidence of what they think is managerial incompetence. Do shareholders need such a watchdog committee as a kind of shadow board to protect their interests, or can this task be undertaken by the larger institutional shareholders?

Shareholders, like the companies in which they invest, come in all sizes. The reasons given above which make it difficult for an individual shareholder with a modest holding in a number of companies to follow their affairs closely can hardly be said to be relevant to the position of large institutional shareholders or the managers of investment trusts. It might be thought that the individual small investor could shelter safely under the wing of the large institutional shareholder who can command a good deal of professional investment expertise, but to date this has not usually been the case. The largely passive role of the big institutions, for which they now find themselves reproached, is an interesting example of the reluctance of certain types of companies to use their considerable powers, or at any rate to be seen using them, for fear of an unfavourable public reaction. If some form of shareholders' committees were to be created with a view to improving the efficiency of companies when they were suspected of operating substantially below their potential, large institutional shareholders could play a very significant role in them. Even if it were possible with the support of the institutional shareholders to elect a committee, the real difficulty would still remain: how could its members have the kind of access to the company's inmost affairs in a way which would enable them, without disclosure harmful to the company's and therefore their own interests, to pronounce upon the merits or otherwise of the board's management? A proposal for setting up shareholders' committees under certain circumstances has recently been the subject of a Private Members' Bill which reached a

Second Reading.[1] This meets the usual objections to such committees by accepting that, once constituted, they need professional advice in the shape of independent management consultants who may be instructed to carry out a thorough management audit into all or part of the company's business. Their audit would not be carried out to check the accuracy and probity of companies' accounts, but to report to the committee on the efficiency with which the company is using its resources. The Bill was not intended to encourage the vexatious intervention in a company's affairs of a few dissident shareholders, and indeed its sponsors hoped that its effect would be to encourage managements to forestall the shareholders by calling in management consultants themselves. Though the idea is not without some practical objections it is a valuable opening proposal in the search for more effective control of company boards by shareholders.

There are of course institutional factors which cause company boards to serve shareholders' interests even if they do not have them consciously in mind: for example, the activities of possible takeover bidders, and the well-publicized judgements of investment analysts and financial journalists. Treating shareholders' interests as paramount in law can never produce a *close* control of company boards' behaviour; but despite the imperfections of the system, it does seem to offer over the long run a fair working accommodation of non-shareholder interests.

Thus a good many of the situations which might appear to involve conflicts of interest requiring to be balanced are resolved by market forces, by law and, over the long term, by coincidence of benefit. However, there may remain some conflicts where boards do not believe this to be so, and they may choose to exercise their judgement in favour of consumers, employees or the public interest. The most clear-cut of the cases where there may be such conflicts would seem to be those where the company does not have a long-term future, because it is about to be taken over or liquidated. Some lawyers have pointed out that if directors are to see conflicts of interest as being resolved over the long term by coincidence of benefit, this view must be based on a presumption of the continuity of the enterprise. They question whether the present legal framework leaves room for that presumption and suggest that problems arise if that presumption is invalidated by a contemplated cessation of the continuity. In cases

[1] *Bill to amend the law relating to Companies so as to require that the agenda of annual general meetings shall include, upon special notice, consideration of the appointment of shareholders' representative committees,* H. of C. Bill No. 166, 1st reading, 21 May 1969. Subsequently amended in Standing Committee 16 July, and renumbered H. of C. Bill No. 200.

where boards believe long-term conflicts do exist, and where they wish to resolve them in favour of interests other than the shareholders, the question arises as to whether there needs to be some reformulation of company law to remove doubts as to the legality of their actions. Alternatively or additionally, does a code of good practice need to be devised to guide company boards in their use of these discretionary powers, which will make more clear than is now the case to whom they are accountable when boards allocate company resources to non-profit-seeking activities?

Chapter 8

Conclusions

There was a general agreement among the boards of the large companies consulted in this study that they have social responsibilities, and they tended to identify these in the areas of employee welfare, more democratic styles of management, corporate philanthropy and in general a concern for the social consequences of their business activities in such matters as pollution and industrial location, etc.

None of the companies had any doubts that their primary objective was to be efficient and profitable and that being socially responsible would serve no useful purpose if it hindered these overall company goals. But they recognized that some activities, apparently non-profit-seeking in the short run, might be a necessary part of longer-term business success and therefore in no way in conflict with the ongoing prosperity of the company and its ability to serve the best interests of the shareholders.

Examined more closely the greater part of the policies described by companies as ways of meeting what they conceived to be their responsibilities was in fact founded on enlightened business interest. Generous fringe benefits, responsible redundancy policies and the obligation to declare and adhere to company objectives were all ways in which management hoped for a more co-operative industrial climate both inside and outside their factories. In some companies this was seen simply as more intelligent management because it was a more appropriate form of management in contemporary social circumstances. In other boardrooms the emphasis lay more in meeting the rightful claims of employees to have a greater share, as members of the company, in the organization of their work. The most democratic form of company management, as regards the relations between managers and board, encountered among companies consulted was in a small but rapidly growing private company whose managing director believed that this was not only the most efficient method of running the company, but that it was also the best method of training the managers needed to take over the direction of other organizations being absorbed by his company. In both cases boards were responding to what they thought were social expectations about how companies ought to behave to their employees, and both expected that the results of such policies would be to enable them to run the company more successfully for all concerned.

These general good intentions were weakened in some companies first by the rather paternalistic pattern of industrial welfare in which developments were initiated and controlled largely if not entirely by management, and which were assumed without consultation to be meeting employees' needs. Secondly, social and business objectives were not clearly distinguished and the results of investing resources for social purposes were not subject to the kind of follow-up and testing which would have been applied in the same companies to business investments. Social policies were assumed to be serving laudable purposes without much effort to measure their effects.

For company spokesmen in this study, socially responsible behaviour to employees and the community at large seemed to be regarded as an obligation, a sort of *noblesse oblige*, which went with industrial importance, and activities undertaken for these reasons seemed very congenial to those on the management side who were involved. Individual companies expected to pioneer new developments in the future and to continue to derive satisfaction from giving a lead to their industry or to business generally, as much in fields of industrial welfare as in product innovation.

One area of company activity which was commonly accepted as a social duty, the making of company donations, did not appear to coincide so neatly with business objectives. Although some company donations are given for specific or general business reasons, some have no apparent connection with business needs, and this raises the question of what are the grounds for this kind of allocation of company resources. Convention, lack of shareholder objection, and the presumed social value of gathering funds from many independent sources for socially-useful purposes have hallowed the custom of corporate charitable giving so that its legality and propriety are no longer seriously questioned. Indeed a strong case can be made out for asking companies to give more, and to give in a more positive and informed way. However this does raise the question of the scale of company giving. There are not likely to be widespread objections to a substantial increase above the present level in Britain; and indeed there is much to be said for a measure of pluralism in the support of some activities which are otherwise dependent almost entirely on government finance. But if donations were to be increased very substantially (e.g. to more than 5 per cent of net income), not only might shareholders object, but it might also be claimed (as has already happened in America) that corporate giving, especially if concentrated in company-sponsored foundations, would enable these bodies to wield too great an influence on social policies. The wisdom of allowing companies to exercise very great influence, underwritten by public funds in the shape of fiscal concessions, might be questioned if they were giving or withholding support for developments more properly considered to be the province of governments.

The most difficult problem arising from this concept of company board responsibilities, as the companies themselves believed, was the demand that they should seek to serve the public interest. This was not because they were unwilling to do so—on the contrary, most of them described their business activities as serving the public—but because they did not want to be under pressure from government or its agencies to conform to concepts of public interest laid down by them. If it is accepted that above and beyond any requirements of law, company boards must serve the public interest, they fear that this may mean an increasing power for governments to direct company policies, since the Government is the only properly constituted authority which can pronounce upon what is or is not in the public interest. Company reformers are divided into a number of groups because they envisage different functions for the modern corporation. Those who believe companies must more positively recognize their social obligations offer different remedies from those who are concerned about the need for a closer control of companies in order to try to make them more efficient, since they believe that in this lies the true responsibility of company boards to the community at large. Theories of the firm and empirical studies of business behaviours have tended to throw doubt on profit-maximizing either as the sole intention or the effect of company activities. Increments in the size of firm, since these are likely to lead to increases in salary and status for the managers inside the company, may be pursued in a way which does not secure an optimum return to shareholders. Or, on the other hand, managers concerned with job security and perhaps a quiet life[1] may have no incentive for risky innovations, and may deliberately sacrifice some part of what might have been a return to shareholders for a non-pecuniary benefit within the firm. It has been suggested[2] that these may include 'pretty secretaries, thick rugs, friendly colleagues, leisurely work loads, executive washrooms, larger work staff, relaxed personnel policies involving job security, time off for statesmanlike community activities, gifts of company funds to

[1] P. W. S. Andrews and Elisabeth Brunner, 'Business Profits and the Quiet Life', *Journal of Industrial Economics*, November 1962.

[2] Armen A. Alchian, 'The Basis of Some Recent Advances in the Theory of Management of the Firm', *Journal of Industrial Economics*, November 1965.

college', etc. On this view some non-profit-seeking activities such as making company donations are one of the pleasant duties of office enjoyed by company directors.

If the long-term maximizing of profits is to remain the overriding goal of companies, and if the formula of the balance of interests does not itself offer any clear guide to company decision-making, what are the factors that can make companies more clearly accountable and, if this is desired, more socially responsible without at the same time impairing their efficiency? There are three approaches through which some changes might be brought about: first by changing the legal framework within which companies operate; secondly, by strengthening the institutional factors which press companies to improve their performance; and, thirdly, by evolving new norms of corporate behaviour which companies will be willing to impose upon themselves.

The first is in the province of company lawyers, but it is to be hoped that changes in the law can, without hobbling enterprise, deal with two important needs. One is to tighten up the law to prevent fraud and the reckless use of company resources. This would mean constantly reviewing company law in order to check abuses as they develop, and thus to prevent the misuse of the corporate form for purposes such as tax evasion. Secondly, legal obligations laid on companies, of which some of the most important are concerned with disclosure of their activities, might include provision for the right, under certain circumstances, for duly authorized representatives of shareholders to satisfy themselves about the true state of a company's affairs by commissioning an independent progress report in addition to that provided by the board itself. The cost of policing management (which, if excessive, cancels out its value to shareholders) would set limits to an over-resort to this kind of procedure, but its existence might act as a powerful check on companies even if not often invoked. Thus there are grounds, in the context of reform of the company law, for considering the establishment of shareholders' committees (which could be called supervisory boards), as suggested in the previous chapter.

The institutional factors which make companies both more competitive and more circumspect in their dealings with the various interest groups with which they are concerned are already stronger than is sometimes supposed and could be further strengthened. The salutary effects, for example, of some recent mergers may serve *pour encourager les autres*, since for every merger that takes place there are an unknown number of companies which reappraise and subsequently try to improve their own position. Also it must not be

167

overlooked that one of the most important aspects of competition especially in large companies is internal competition, that is the struggle which goes on inside a company. If product divisions have to demonstrate their profitability in order to compete successfully for their share of company resources, and the promotion and salary structure allows the most able people in the company to get into the top jobs, it may not matter whether individual businessmen are concerned with seeking their own advancement or any other personal objectives and satisfactions including being socially responsible, as long as this is consistent with the overall goals of the company.

If social responsibility is to be a legitimate concern of corporate behaviour, how is this to be defined? Can boards be allowed to make their own definitions of their obligations or ought something more precise to be devised, capable perhaps of embodiment ultimately if not immediately in company law? A number of companies have drawn up statements (as did the company in the case study described in Chapter 4) setting out company objective. The International Publishing Corporation, for example, has recently devoted a good deal of top executive time to drafting and making known throughout the company a statement in which the company recognized the need to take into account the interests of employees and the public interest. The company accepts that its business must be carried on 'within the context set by the social obligations of the time' and defines these as 'the moral, ethical and other obligations which at any particular time are considered to be relevant'. Companies consulted in this study were divided in their views on the value of such statements. Some thought it useful to state positively that they recognized the social as well as economic purposes of their organization, while others felt that such statements tended to consist of pious platitudes and begged a great many of the really difficult questions. With or without this kind of 'managerial ten commandments'[1] many companies do already impose some non-statutory duties upon themselves. Can they be relied upon to meet social obligations voluntarily? Left to their own devices, a very uneven and diverse pattern emerges, but this is often offered as a major justification for the use of company resources for social purposes: it permits a pluralist approach claimed to be preferable to the exclusive use of uniform state action. Experiment and innovation are said to be possible in meeting community needs in this way and a general improvement in employee welfare can be gradually extended from the pioneer and demonstration projects of leading companies.

[1] M. P. Fogarty, *A Company Act 1970?* PEP Broadsheet No. 500, October 1967.

How much of this kind of non-profit-making behaviour should be expected from companies and, if companies are to decide this for themselves, how do they set about making their decisions? While it is hoped that the analysis of our study material will shed useful light on these policy problems, our research did not discover any simple formulae for directors to apply—perhaps, indeed, the nature of the problem is such that no simple formula is applicable. The research showed, rather, that the company boards studied are seeking socially acceptable forms of behaviour, and sometimes going beyond what is socially expected where they judge that this will be acceptable to the company's owners. Both directors and owners appear to share in the general climate of public opinion about what it is reasonable for companies to do in the way of looking after their employees, or making charitable gifts or protecting public amenities, and thus accept some non-pecuniary satisfaction. For example, there is no evidence of shareholder objections to donations now they are disclosed, or to improvements in conditions for employees when reported. Thus a successful company may judge that it needs to be aware of social demands for new forms of corporate responsibility as much as it needs to respond to demands for new products. Indeed, quite apart from the laying of new legal obligations on companies, new developments are all the time taking place in their policies. In the area of provision for redundant employees for example, which is a problem of special difficulty during a period of industrial change, some companies are moving ahead of their statutory duties. An example of this is the recent creation of an organization called the New Opportunities Association which has been sponsored by a dozen large companies. This is an independent non-profit-making bureau supported by subscriptions and fees paid by employers per item of service, which tries to place redundant employees. In this way the companies demonstrate that they recognize that redundancy and severance pay and other forms of financial compensation are only a partial answer to the problems some of their former employees, perhaps now middle-aged, have in finding work, and in this way these companies show that they accept a positive responsibility to help their redundant staff find suitable new jobs.

If the social responsibilities of company boards are seen as a general responsiveness to the changing social climate in which business activities are carried on, and from which companies cannot insulate themselves, organized labour, alert consumer associations and informed public opinion can be expected to create social pressures which will effect desired changes, albeit slowly, in company practices. If, on the other hand, making companies responsible is believed to mean that they must be made more accountable to bodies on which not only shareholders but employees and consumers and the general public are directly and evenly represented, then new legal forms will have to be devised. For the reasons set out in Chapter 7 this would present formidable difficulties for which satisfactory solutions do not as yet appear to have been found.

Index